Teacher's Resource Masters

VOLUME 1

Topics 1–8

Home-School Connection Letters
Math and Science Activities
Daily Common Core Review
Reteach to Build Understanding
Center Games
Fluency Practice/Assessment

enVisionmath 2.0
SCOTT FORESMAN · ADDISON WESLEY

PEARSON

Glenview, Illinois • Boston, Massachusetts • Chandler, Arizona • Hoboken, New Jersey

ISBN-13: 978-0-328-82762-6
ISBN-10: 0-328-82762-2
2 3 4 5 6 7 8 9 10 11 V0N4 19 18 17 16 15

Grade 6
Volume 1: Topics 1–8

Topic 5   **Algebra: Patterns and Equations**

Topic 6   **Fluently Divide Whole Numbers**

Topic 7   **Fluently Add, Subtract, Multiply, and Divide Decimals**

Topic 8   **Common Factors and Multiples**

Algebra: Understand Numerical and Algebraic Expressions

Topic 1 Standards

6.EE.A.1, 6.EE.A.2a, 6.EE.A.2b, 6.EE.A.2c, 6.EE.A.3, 6.EE.A.4, 6.EE.B.6

See the front of the Student's Edition for complete standards.

Dear Family,

Your child is learning how to read, write, and evaluate expressions that represent situations and patterns, and how to use order of operations and properties when evaluating expressions. He or she will use variables to represent numbers and write expressions to solve real-world and mathematical problems.

Suppose your son or daughter has grown 2 inches since the last time he or she was measured. To represent your child's current height, you could use the variable h to represent the previous height and add 2. So, the expression $h + 2$ would represent your child's current height. To evaluate the expression, you would substitute your child's previous height for h.

Here is an activity you can try to help your child learn how to write and evaluate expressions.

Household Expressions

One way to help your child develop skills in writing and evaluating expressions is to write expressions for everyday situations, and then evaluate the expressions for different numbers. Here are some typical situations you might use.

Food Preparation: What expression can you use to show dividing some pancakes among 4 family members? ($p \div 4$, where p is the number of pancakes)

Chores: What expression can you use to show the total amount of time it takes to do chores, if it takes 20 minutes to do each chore? ($20c$ or $20 \times c$, where c is the number of chores)

Observe Your Child

Focus on Mathematical Practice 4
Model with mathematics.

Help your child become proficient with Mathematical Practice 4. When working with expressions with your child, make sure that he or she names and defines the variable before writing the expression. Stress that once a variable has been chosen, it represents the same measure throughout the situation.

Nombre _____

Álgebra: Expresiones numéricas y algebraicas

Estándares del Tema 1

6.EE.A.1, 6.EE.A.2a, 6.EE.A.2b, 6.EE.A.2c, 6.EE.A.3, 6.EE.A.4, 6.EE.B.6

Los estándares completos se encuentran en las páginas preliminares del Libro del estudiante.

Estimada familia:

Su niño(a) está aprendiendo a leer, escribir y evaluar expresiones que representan situaciones y patrones, y a usar el orden de las operaciones y las propiedades al evaluar expresiones. Usará variables para representar cantidades y escribirá expresiones para resolver problemas matemáticos de la vida diaria.

Supongan que su hijo(a) creció 2 pulgadas desde la última vez que lo (la) midieron. Para representar su altura actual, podrían usar la variable a para representar la altura anterior y sumar 2. Entonces, la expresión $a + 2$ representaría la altura actual de su hijo(a). Para evaluar esta expresión, podrían sustituir la altura anterior de su hijo(a) por a.

Pruebe esta actividad con su niño(a) para aprender a escribir y evaluar expresiones.

Expresiones familiares

Una forma de ayudar a su niño(a) a desarrollar destrezas en la escritura y la evaluación de expresiones es escribir expresiones para situaciones de la vida diaria y, luego, evaluarlas con distintos valores. Aquí hay algunas situaciones que podrían ser útiles.

Preparación en la cocina: ¿Qué expresión puedes utilizar para representar el reparto de unos panqueques entre 4 integrantes de la familia? ($p \div 4$, donde p es la cantidad de panqueques)

Tareas domésticas: ¿Qué expresión puedes usar para representar el total de tiempo que toma realizar las tareas domésticas si toma 20 minutos hacer cada una? ($20t$ o $20 \times t$, donde t es la cantidad de tareas domésticas).

Observe a su niño(a)

Enfoque en la Práctica matemática 4
Representar modelos matemáticos.

Ayude a su niño(a) a adquirir competencia en la Práctica matemática 4. Al trabajar con expresiones, asegúrese de que su niño(a) identifique y defina la variable antes de escribir la expresión. Enfatice que una vez que se elige una variable, debe representar la misma medida durante todo el proceso.

Name _____

Energy Transfer in an Ecosystem

Did You Know? Only 10% of the energy at one level of a food chain is transferred to the next higher level. The other 90% is converted to heat energy. As a result, there are fewer organisms at the highest level in a food chain.

1 In an ecosystem, some animals get energy by eating other animals. An adult barn owl eats up to 6 mice each day. An owlet eats about 1.5 mice each day. Write and evaluate an expression to find how many mice are eaten in one week by 2 adult barn owls and 6 owlets.

_____

2 **Represent** The average female mouse gives birth to 5 to 10 litters per year. There are 5 to 6 young mice per litter. What is the fewest number of mice an average female could give birth to in one year? What is the greatest number? Write a numerical expression to show the difference between these high and low birth numbers. How many terms are in your expression? Then evaluate your expression.

_____

_____

_____

3 **Extension** How many reproducing female mice will produce enough offspring to feed one barn owl for a year? Choose the number of mice the owl will eat daily. Then use the information from Problem 2 to estimate the number of mice a female produces in one year. Write and evaluate an expression that shows how to calculate a reasonable answer.

_____

_____

_____

Name _____

Nature's Recyclers

> **Did You Know?** The atoms that make up all organisms in an ecosystem are repeatedly cycled between the living and nonliving parts. *Decomposers*—bacteria, mold, and mushrooms—return simple molecules to the environment by consuming the waste and remains of other organisms.

Each student in Mr. Lee's class fills a box with a soil sample. The students will test their soil to identify decomposers. The sample boxes are cubes of various sizes. Use the formulas below to answer the questions. In both formulas, the variable *s* represents the length of a side of the cube. The length, width, and height of a cube are all equal.

$$\text{Volume of a cube: } V = s^3$$
$$\text{Surface area of a cube: } A = 6s^2$$

1 One sample box has sides measuring 30 cm each. Write the volume as a power of 10 with an exponent. Show your work.

_____

2 A small sample box has sides measuring 10 cm each. Write the surface area in standard form. Show your work.

_____

3 **Represent** Soil weighs 1.32 grams per cubic centimeter. Write an algebraic expression that Mr. Lee's students could use to show the mass of the soil in any sample box. Use your expression to find the mass of soil in the sample box in Exercise 2.

_____

4 **Extension** A gram of soil can contain 3 billion bacteria and 1 million fungi, which include yeasts and molds. Write a numerical expression to represent the number of these organisms in the sample box from Exercise 2. Use powers of 10 in your expression.

_____

Name _____

1. How many feet are in 9 yards?

Ⓐ 3 feet

Ⓑ 6 feet

Ⓒ 9 feet

Ⓓ 27 feet

2. What is the place value of the underlined digit?
5.2<u>3</u>6

Ⓐ Tenths

Ⓑ Hundredths

Ⓒ Thousandths

Ⓓ Ones

3. Which of the following numbers would be farthest to the right on a number line?

Ⓐ 162.662

Ⓑ 162.226

Ⓒ 16.772

Ⓓ 16.426

4. Evaluate this expression.
$(4 \times 30) + (4 \times 3)$

Ⓐ 12,012

Ⓑ 1,320

Ⓒ 132

Ⓓ 120

5. Write the numbers below in order from least to greatest.
1.4   10.4   1.45   1.54   10.54

_____

_____

6. Amy has 8 yards of fabric. How many pillows can she make if she uses $\frac{1}{3}$ yard of fabric for each pillow?

_____

7. What is 0.25×20?

_____

8. If the upward trend on the graph below continues, what will be the next point plotted?

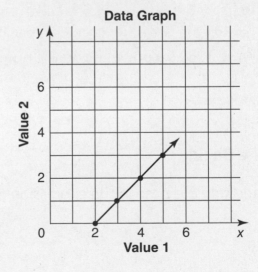

_____

Vocabulary

1. An **exponent** can be used to write a repeated multiplication expression, such as $2 \times 2 \times 2 \times 2 = 2^4$. The exponent tells how many times a number is used as a factor.

   Write the exponent. $3 \times 3 \times 3 \times 3 \times 3 = 3^{\square}$

2. The number that is repeatedly multiplied is the **base**.

   What is the base in the expression 3^5? _____

3. A number that can be written using exponents is a **power**. Use repeated multiplication to **evaluate,** or find the value of, a power.

   Evaluate 2^3. _____

4. What is the exponent in the expression 6^4? _____

5. Evaluate the expression.

   10^3 _____

6. Write 125 as a repeated multiplication of 5s.

   _____

7. Write 125 as a power using the number 5 as the base.

   _____

On the Back!

8. Identify the base in the expression 6^{10}.

Display the Digits

Get Started
👤 or 👥

Explain how to answer the question.
Display each 0–9 tile exactly once.
If you have a partner, take turns.

a. What is the value of 5^0?

b. What would be the exponent if $4 \times 4 \times 4$ were written as a power?

c. The value of any power with this exponent is always 1.

d. Which digit is the base in 2^7?

e. Which digit is the exponent in 2^8?

f. What would be the exponent if $0.5 \times 0.5 \times 0.5 \times 0.5$ were written as a power?

g. If $6 \times 6 \times 6$ were written using an exponent, what would be the base?

h. Which number is the exponent in $\left(\frac{2}{3}\right)^5$?

i. What is the value of 7^1?

j. What is the value of 3^2?

If you have more time

Make up other questions about exponents.
Ask your partner to display the answers with 0–9 tiles.

Center Game ★ 1·1

Display the Digits

Partner Talk

Share your thinking while you work.

 **Get Started**

Explain how to answer the question.
Display each 0–9 tile exactly once.
If you have a partner, take turns.

a. What is the value of the missing exponent that would make this statement true? $256^? = 256$

b. Which number is the exponent in 2.3^6?

c. Which digit is the base in 7^5?

d. What would be the exponent if $3 \times 3 \times 3 \times 3 \times 3$ were written as a power?

e. What is the value of 8×7^0?

f. What would be the exponent if $\frac{1}{2} \times \frac{1}{2} \times \frac{1}{2} \times \frac{1}{2}$ were written as a power?

g. What is the value of $3 \times (0.3)^0$?

h. What is the value of the missing exponent that would make this statement true? $3^0 = 5^?$

i. If $9 \times 9 \times 9 \times 9$ were written using an exponent, what would be the base?

j. A base number is raised to an exponent of 4 and the result is 16. What is the value of the base number?

 **If you have more time**

Make up other questions about exponents.
Ask your partner to display the answers with 0–9 tiles.

Center Game ★★ **1·1**

1. Ted bought a CD for $18.95 and a ball cap for $14.95. He also paid $2.37 in sales tax. How much did Ted pay for the two items including tax?

   Ⓐ $33.90

   Ⓑ $36.27

   Ⓒ $36.28

   Ⓓ $57.63

2. Manny built a chest shaped like a rectangular solid. The base was 10 inches long and 6 inches wide. It had a height of 4 inches. What is the volume of the chest?

   Ⓐ 60 in.^{2}

   Ⓑ 60 in.^{3}

   Ⓒ 240 in.^{2}

   Ⓓ 240 in.^{3}

3. Which of the following expressions are equal to 125? Select all that apply.

   ☐ 3^5

   ☐ 5^3

   ☐ $625 \div 5$

   ☐ $3 \times 3 \times 3 \times 3 \times 3$

   ☐ $5 \times 5 \times 5$

4. Evaluate 8^4.

   Ⓐ 32

   Ⓑ 512

   Ⓒ 4,096

   Ⓓ 32,768

The graph shows the relationship between how fast dogs age and how fast humans age. The first two years of a dog's life are equivalent to 10.5 human years each. The other years of a dog's life are each equivalent to 4 human years.

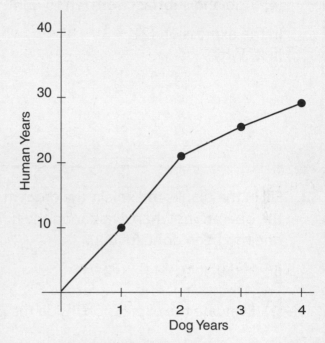

5. What information is represented by the ordered pair (3, 25)?

   _____

   _____

   _____

   _____

6. Using this relationship, find the equivalent age in human years of a dog that has lived 12 years.

   _____

Name _____

A-Z Vocabulary

1. The **order of operations** is a set of rules to follow when evaluating expressions.

   Order of Operations
   (1) Evaluate expressions in parentheses and brackets from the inside out.
   (2) Evaluate powers.
   (3) Multiply and divide from left to right.
   (4) Add and subtract from left to right.

   In the expression $(21 - 3) \div 6 + 9^2$, what operation should you perform first? Why?

   _____

   _____

2. Fill in the blanks to explain the order in which you would perform the operations when evaluating the following expression. The first one has been done for you.

   $6^2 + [(59 - 4) \div 11] \times 2$

   (1) Evaluate the expression inside the parentheses by subtracting.

   (2) _____

   (3) _____

   (4) _____

   (5) _____

3. Evaluate the expression $6^2 + [(59 - 4) \div 11] \times 2$ by following the steps you wrote.

   _____

On the Back!

4. Use the order of operations to evaluate the expression $(11^2 - 21) \times \left(\frac{1}{2}\right)^2 + 5$. Show your work.

Toss and Talk

 **Get Started**

or

Get 10 squares in one color and 10 in another color.
Get two number cubes. Take turns with another player or team.
Talk about math as you play!

At Your Turn

Toss two number cubes. Add the dots. Find your toss below.
Follow the directions. Explain your thinking. Cover the answer.
If the answer is taken, lose your turn. Have fun!

Toss	Explain how to use the correct order of operations to evaluate the expression. You may use paper and a pencil.
2	$[(2^3 \times 2.5) \div 4] + 1.3$
3	$4^2 - [44.4 \div 11.1] \times 3$
4	$3^2 + [(15 - 7) \times 4.5]$
5	$[2 \times (75 \div 3)] - 3^3$
6	$6^2 - 18 \times \frac{1}{3}$

7	$2^4 - [(33.3 \div 11.1) \times \frac{1}{3}]$
8	$(8.3 + 3.7) \times \left(\frac{1}{2}\right)^2$
9	$7.6 - (3^2 \div 3) \times 2$
10	$5.3 \times [(2^2 \times 3.5) \div 7]$
11	$[(3 + 3^2) - 5.1] + 2.6$
12	$2.9 + [8.1 \times \left(\frac{1}{3}\right)^2] \times 3$

1.6	6.3	3	9.5
45	15	23	30
30	4	10.6	1.6
23	3	15	5.6

How to Win — You win if you are the first to get four connected rectangles, like:

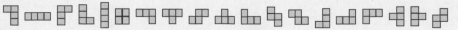

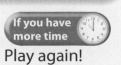 **If you have more time** Play again!

Center Game ★ 1·2

6

Toss and Talk

Partner Talk

Share your thinking while you work.

Get Started or

Get 10 squares in one color and 10 in another color.
Get two number cubes. Take turns with another player or team.
Talk about math as you play!

At Your Turn

Toss two number cubes. Add the dots. Find your toss below.
Follow the directions. Explain your thinking. Cover the answer.
If the answer is taken, lose your turn. Have fun!

Toss	Explain how to use the correct order of operations to evaluate the expression. You may use paper and a pencil.
2	$6^3 \times \left(\frac{1}{3}\right)^2 - 3 \times 5$
3	$5.4 \div 3^2 + 3 - 1.6$
4	$4.5 \div 3^2 + 4^2 \times \left(\frac{1}{2}\right)^2$
5	$5 - 0.2^2 \times 20 + 1$
6	$32 - 45 \times \left(\frac{1}{3}\right)^2$

7	$2.3^2 + 5 \times 2$
8	$105 \div 7 + 2^3$
9	$2.5 \times 2 + 3.4 - 1.6$
10	$4 \times 3.2 - 7.2 \div 2^3$
11	$24 \div 2^2 + 2.6 \times \frac{1}{2}$
12	$2^2 \times 5 - 12 \times \left(\frac{1}{2}\right)^2$

4.5	23	17	27
7.3	15.29	5.2	9
9	7.3	27	6.8
5.2	2	15.29	11.9

How to Win

You win if you are the first to get four connected rectangles, like:

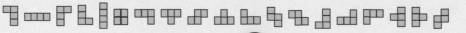

If you have more time
Play again!

Name _____

1. Which of the following has a value of 10?

   (A) $12 \div (2 + 5 - 1)$

   (B) $(12 \div 2) + (5 - 1)$

   (C) $(12 - 2) \div 5 + 1$

   (D) $12 \div (5 + 1) + 2$

2. Which shows the decimals in order from least to greatest?

   (A) 3.001, 3.01, 3.1, 3.101

   (B) 3.001, 3.01, 3.101, 3.1

   (C) 3.01, 3.001, 3.101, 3.1

   (D) 3.1, 3.01, 3.001, 3.101

3. Write $6 \times 6 \times 6 \times 6$ using exponents.

   (A) 4^6

   (B) 6^4

   (C) 4×6

   (D) 6×4

4. A coordinate grid has two points. One point is at (16, 5). The other point is two units down and five units to the left. Which ordered pair names that point?

   (A) (11, 3)

   (B) (14, 0)

   (C) (18, 10)

   (D) (21, 7)

5. The Anderson family's May phone bill is shown below.

Phone Bill	
Monthly Fee	$29.50
$0.05 per minute for 3,200 minutes	$160.00
Total for May	$189.50

The Andersons used 1,600 minutes of phone time in June. Mr. Anderson explained how he found the amount of the June phone bill below.

> **Mr. Anderson's Solution**
> For 3,200 min, I paid $189.50. We used 1,600 min in June, which is $\frac{1}{2}$ of 3,200 min. So, the bill for June will be $\frac{1}{2}$ of $189.50, or $94.75.

Is Mr. Anderson correct? Explain.

_____

_____

_____

_____

_____

_____

_____

_____

D 1·3

Name _____

(A-Z) Vocabulary

1. A **variable** is a letter or symbol that represents an unknown quantity. An **algebraic expression** is an expression that has one or more variables and at least one operation.

   Identify the variable and the operation(s) in each algebraic expression.

Algebraic Expression	Variable	Operation(s)
$7 + m$		
$p - 12$		
$15w$		
$\frac{c}{8}$		
$2(h + 15)$		

2. Write an algebraic expression for each situation.

   twenty less than a number n _____

   the sum of fifteen and a number b _____

   the quotient of twenty-four divided by a number g _____

   six more than the quantity d times two _____

3. Luca works at a grocery store on the weekends. He earns $8.50 per hour.

   Choose a variable to represent the number of hours Luca works. _____

   What operation can be used to find the total amount Luca earns? _____

   Write an algebraic expression to represent the total amount Luca earns from working at the grocery store. _____

On the Back!

4. Write an algebraic expression for three times the quantity q minus eleven.

Clip and Cover

Get Started  Get 10 squares in one color and 10 in another color, two paper clips, and two number cubes. Take turns.

At Your Turn Toss two cubes to find your ovals. **EXAMPLE:** Choose the 3rd oval on the left and the 5th oval on the right, **or** choose the 5th oval on the left and the 3rd oval on the right. Mark your ovals with paper clips.

How to Play Read the word phrase in your left oval followed by the word phrase in your right oval. Find the corresponding algebraic expression. Explain your choice. Cover the answer. Lose your turn if the answer is taken.

How to Win The first player or team to get any three connected rectangles in a row or column wins.

Left ovals					Right ovals
10 less than	$4s - 10$	$8c - 10$	$n \div 15 - 8.5$	$10 \times 4s$	4 times a number s
10 more than	$10 \times \dfrac{100}{k}$	$100 \div k - 10$	$4s - 8.5$	$\dfrac{100}{k} - 8.5$	a number n divided by 15
8.5 fewer than	$10 \times \dfrac{n}{15}$	$8c - 8.5$	$100 \div k + 10$	$8c + 10$	8 times a number c
10 times	$\dfrac{n}{15} - 10$	$4s + 10$	$n \div 15 + 10$	$10 \times 8c$	100 divided by a number k
10 added to					a number c times 8
8.5 less than					a number n divided by 15

If you have more time  Play again! Does what you read first always appear first in the algebraic expression? Why not?

Center Game ★ 1·3

Clip and Cover

Partner Talk

Share your thinking while you work.

 **Get Started** ∱∱ or ∱∱∱
Get 10 squares in one color and 10 in another color, one paper clip, and one number cube. Take turns.

At Your Turn
Toss one cube to find your oval. **EXAMPLE:** ⚁ Choose the 3rd oval on the left, **or** choose the 3rd oval on the right. Mark your oval with a paper clip.

How to Play
The variable in the algebraic expression you chose represents a number.
Say a word phrase for your algebraic expression.
Cover that word phrase. Lose your turn if the answer is taken.

How to Win
The first player or team to get any three connected rectangles in a row or column wins.

Left ovals					Right ovals
$3s - 15$	15 less than 3 times a number	$\frac{1}{2}$ less than a number divided by 5	a number increased by 20	2 less than 13 times a number	$x + 20$
$6(h \div 3)$	5 more than the quotient of a number divided by 4	5 times the quotient of a number divided by 2	25 more than 4 times a number	the sum of 2 and the quantity 7 times a number	$4x + 25$
$r \div 5.75$	1 more than 7 divided by a number	2 more than 7 times a number	6 times the quotient of a number divided by 3	3 times a number minus 15	$\frac{b}{5} - \frac{1}{2}$
$7k + 2$	a number divided by 5.75	the sum of 25 and the quantity 4 times a number	13 times a number decreased by 2	13 less than twice a number	$\frac{s}{4} + 5$
$5(r \div 2)$					$13x - 2$
$7 \div m + 1$					$2x - 13$

 **If you have more time**
Play again! Talk about your strategies as you play.

Center Game ★★ 1·3

1. Which of the following expresses the quantity of *w* watermelon slices divided among 6 children?

   Ⓐ $6 \div w$

   Ⓑ $w \div 6$

   Ⓒ $6w$

   Ⓓ $w - 6$

2. Which algebraic expression represents a number *h* subtracted from 5?

   Ⓐ $5 + h$

   Ⓑ $h - 5$

   Ⓒ $h \times 5$

   Ⓓ $5 - h$

3. What is the standard form for thirteen and four hundred six thousandths?

   Ⓐ 13.046

   Ⓑ 13.460

   Ⓒ 13.4006

   Ⓓ 13.406

4. Evaluate the expression $2^3 + (18 - 3) \div 3$.

   Ⓐ 7

   Ⓑ 13

   Ⓒ 15

   Ⓓ 25

5. Write an expression for 5 times a number.

   _____

6. In each of the last 3 weeks, Maria ran 3 miles on each of 3 days. Write the number of miles Maria ran in all using exponents and in standard form.

   using exponents: _____

   standard form: _____

7. Jill has two bags of marbles. The first bag weighs 2 pounds 6 ounces and the second bag weighs 40 ounces. Which bag of marbles weighs more? Explain.

   _____

   _____

   _____

   _____

8. What is the volume of the rectangular prism?

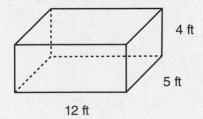

   4 ft

   5 ft

   12 ft

   _____

Vocabulary

1. A **term** of a mathematical expression is a part that is separated by a plus or minus sign. $3q - \frac{q}{4} + 4 \cdot 5$ has three terms. The terms are $3q$, $\frac{q}{4}$, and $4 \cdot 5$.

   What are the terms of $3.5d - (12 \div 3) + \frac{d}{2}$?

   _____

2. A **coefficient** is the number that is multiplied by a variable. In the term $3q$, the coefficient of q is 3.

   What is the coefficient of d in the term $3.5d$? _____

Answer the following questions to identify the parts of the expression $4.2m + (8 \div 2) - 6$.

3. How many terms does the expression have? _____

4. What are the terms of the expression?

   _____

5. Which term is the product of two factors? _____

   What are the factors of the product? _____

6. Which term is a quotient? _____

   What is the dividend of the quotient? _____

   What is divisor of the quotient? _____

7. Which term is a constant numerical value? _____

On the Back!

8. How many terms does $8 - h$ have? Identify the terms.

Name _____

1. How many terms does the expression
$5^2 + 6 \cdot 2 - 20 \div 4$ have?

   Ⓐ 6

   Ⓑ 5

   Ⓒ 4

   Ⓓ 3

2. In the expression $\frac{x}{5} + 2y - 3$, what is
the coefficient of x?

   Ⓐ 5

   Ⓑ $\frac{1}{5}$

   Ⓒ 2

   Ⓓ −3

3. Which shape is not a parallelogram?

   Ⓐ Square

   Ⓑ Rhombus

   Ⓒ Rectangle

   Ⓓ Trapezoid

4. In what place is the digit 6 in the
number 42.865?

   Ⓐ Thousandths

   Ⓑ Hundredths

   Ⓒ Tenths

   Ⓓ Ones

5. What is the standard form of 7^3?

   _____

6. How many terms does the expression
$3x - \frac{y}{2} + xy - 6$ have?

   _____

7. Which part of the expression
$2(12 + 7) + \frac{5}{8}$ represents a product?

   _____

8. Which part of the expression
$8x - \frac{y + 3}{4} + z$ represents a quotient?

   _____

Evaluate the following expressions using
the order of operations.

9. $4^2 + 18 \div 3 \times 2$

   _____

10. $26 - 9 + (36 \div 3^2)$

   _____

D 1·5

Name _____

Vocabulary

1. When **substitution** is used to evaluate an algebraic expression, a variable is replaced with a number. You can use substitution to find the value of $3a + 4$ when $a = 2$.

   $3a + 4$
   $= 3(2) + 4$ ← Substitute 2 for a.
   $= 6 + 4$ ← Multiply.
   $= 10$ ← Add.

   What is the value of $2x - 1$ when $x = 3$? _____

2. Use substitution to find the value of $m^2 - 2n + \frac{2}{3}p$ when $m = 4$, $n = 2$, and $p = 6$. Use the order of operations to simplify. Fill in the blanks.

   $m^2 - 2n + \frac{2}{3}p$

   $= (\underline{\quad})^2 - 2(\underline{\quad}) + \frac{2}{3}(\underline{\quad})$ ← Substitute the values for each variable.

   $= \underline{\quad} - 2(\underline{\quad}) + \frac{2}{3}(\underline{\quad})$ ← Evaluate powers.

   $= \underline{\quad} - \underline{\quad} + \frac{2}{3}(\underline{\quad})$ ← Multiply.

   $= \underline{\quad} - \underline{\quad} + \underline{\quad}$ ← Multiply.

   $= \underline{\quad} + \underline{\quad}$ ← Subtract.

   $= \underline{\quad}$ ← Add.

3. What is the value of the expression $158 - 8t - (u \div v)$ when $t = 7$,

   $u = 42$, and $v = 6$? _____

On the Back!

4. What is the value of $15b - 2$ when $b = \frac{1}{5}$?

Display the Digits

Partner Talk
Share your thinking while you work.

Get Started  **or**

Explain how to evaluate each expression.
Display each 0–9 tile exactly once.
If you have a partner, take turns.

a. Evaluate $5x - 3$
for $x = 2$.

b. Evaluate $5z - 9 - 2z$
for $z = 4$.

c. Evaluate $2w + 3 + 3w$
for $w = 1$.

d. Evaluate $2g + g + 3g$
$- 5$ for $g = 1$.

e. Evaluate $y^2 - 1$
for $y = 1$.

f. Evaluate $6p + 5 - 3p$
for $p = \frac{1}{3}$.

g. Evaluate $90 - t^2 - 5$
for $t = 9$.

h. Evaluate $5 + \frac{2}{3}a - 4$
for $a = 6$.

i. Evaluate $6r - 3 - 3s$
for $r = 3$ and $s = 2$.

j. Evaluate $3k + 4j - 8$
for $j = 1$ and $k = 2$.

If you have more time
Make up other expressions with a variable.
Ask your partner to display the answers with 0–9 tiles.

Center Game ★ 1·5

Display the Digits

Partner Talk

Share your thinking while you work.

 **Get Started** 👤 or 👤👤

Explain how to evaluate each expression.
Display each 0–9 tile exactly once.
If you have a partner, take turns.

a. Evaluate $(3b + 5) \div (b - 1)$ for $b = 5$.

b. Evaluate $(\frac{1}{3}q^2 - 4) \div (p + 4)$ for $p = 4$ and $q = 6$.

c. Evaluate $(2 + 3c) \times (d - 7)$ for $c = 5$ and $d = 7$.

d. Evaluate $6r^2 + 5r - 1$ for $r = \frac{1}{2}$.

e. Evaluate $4x - (x - \frac{1}{5})$ for $x = \frac{3}{5}$.

f. Evaluate $\frac{1}{2}f + \frac{1}{4}g^2 + 3h$ for $f = 5$, $g = 3$, and $h = \frac{3}{4}$.

g. Evaluate $3t^2 - (8t - 12)$ for $t = 2$.

h. Evaluate $5a + [b - (3c - 4)]$ for $a = 1$, $b = 3$, and $c = 2$.

i. Evaluate $(v + w^2) - (w + 2v - 7)$ for $v = 9$ and $w = 3$.

j. Evaluate $[8x \div (4x - 6)] + (x^2 - 4)$ for $x = 3$.

 **If you have more time**

Make up other expressions with variables.
Ask your partner to display the answers with 0–9 tiles.

Center Game ★★ **1·5**

1. Jason had *s* sea shells. He found 8 more shells. Which expression shows this situation?

   Ⓐ $s + 8$

   Ⓑ $8s$

   Ⓒ $8(s + 8)$

   Ⓓ $s(8 + 8)$

2. Marie's dog lost 4 pounds since the last time she took him to the veterinarian. Which expression shows the current weight of her dog?

   Ⓐ $w - 4$

   Ⓑ $4 - w$

   Ⓒ $4w$

   Ⓓ $w + 4$

3. The table shows the circumference of four trees in the California registry of big trees. Which tree has the least circumference?

Tree	Circumference (ft)
Acacia	9.583
Alder	9.83
Beech	9.917
Weeping Willow	9.67

   Ⓐ Acacia

   Ⓑ Alder

   Ⓒ Beech

   Ⓓ Weeping Willow

4. If $n = 2.5$, what is the value of $n + 3.9$?

   _____

5. How many terms does the expression $3 \cdot 8 - 20 \div 5$ have?

   _____

6. What is the coefficient of x in the expression $\frac{5}{6}x + \frac{2}{3}y - 9$?

   _____

Evaluate the expressions below for $p = 3$.

7. $6p - 16$

   _____

8. $14 + 5p$

   _____

Evaluate the expressions below for $x = 2$, 4, and 7.

9. $3x - 2$

   _____

10. $(x + 8) \div 2$

    _____

Name _____

🅰🅩 Vocabulary

Equivalent expressions have the same value no matter what value is substituted for the same variable in the expressions.

1. Properties of operations can be used to write equivalent expressions. For example, you can show that $2(3x + 1)$ and $6x + 2$ are equivalent expressions by using the Distributive Property and the Associative Property of Multiplication.

   $2(3x + 1)$
   $= 2(3x) + 2(1)$ ← Use the Distributive Property.
   $= (2 \cdot 3)x + 2(1)$ ← Use the Associative Property of Multiplication.
   $= 6x + 2$ ← Multiply.

   What is an equivalent expression for $4(3t - 2)$? _____

2. What is a common factor of both terms in $22m - 33$? _____

3. Rewrite the term $22m$ as a product of 11 and another factor. _____

   Rewrite the term 33 as a product of 11 and another factor. _____

4. Fill in the blanks to write an equivalent expression for $22m - 33$.

   $22m - 33 = 11(\underline{\quad}) - 11(\underline{\quad})$ ← 11 is a common factor.

   $\quad\quad\quad = 11(\underline{\quad} - \underline{\quad})$ ← Use the _____.

5. Write an equivalent expression for each expression below.

   $9z + 27$ $4(w - 5)$ $6(12 - 3b)$ $80 + 20n$

   _____   _____   _____   _____

On the Back!

6. Use properties of operations to write two equivalent expressions for $2(2y - 4)$.

R 1·6

Name _____

1. Which expression is equivalent to $12\left(4a - \frac{5}{6}\right)$?

   Ⓐ $16a - 10$ Ⓒ $48a - 10$

   Ⓑ $48a + 10$ Ⓓ $16a - 12\frac{5}{6}$

2. Evaluate $4^2 + 10 \div 2$.

   Ⓐ 21   Ⓒ 9

   Ⓑ 13   Ⓓ 7

3. What is 100,000 written as a power of 10?

   Ⓐ 10^3 Ⓒ 10^5

   Ⓑ 10^4 Ⓓ 10^6

4. Which of the following is equal to 7?

   Ⓐ $3 \times (2 + 1)$

   Ⓑ $(3 \times 2) + 1$

   Ⓒ $(3 \times 3) - 1$

   Ⓓ $4 + (8 \div 2)$

5. Which of the following is equal to 5^3?

   Ⓐ 5×3

   Ⓑ $3 \times 3 \times 3 \times 3 \times 3$

   Ⓒ $5 + 3$

   Ⓓ $5 \times 5 \times 5$

6. Use the Distributive Property to write an expression that is equivalent to $7(4y - 5)$.

   _____

7. Use the Associative Property of Addition to write an expression that is equivalent to $2x + (3y - 4z)$.

   _____

8. Evaluate the expression for $d = 25$.

   $$d - 12$$

   _____

9. Evaluate the expression $2x + 4$ for $x = 12$.

   _____

10. What is the value of $2x - 3y + z^2$ when $x = 5$, $y = 2$, and $z = 6$?

    _____

11. Michael rode his bike to and from school 3 days last week. If x is the number of miles between Michael's home and school, write an expression to show how many miles Michael rode in all last week.

    _____

12. What is the coefficient of z in the expression $3x + 2y + z$?

    _____

Name _____

Vocabulary

1. **Like terms** are terms that have the same variable part. In the expression $3x - 2y + 5x$, $3x$ and $5x$ are like terms.

   What are the like terms in the expression $3m^2 + 5 - 2m^2$? _____

2. To **simplify** an algebraic expression means to use properties of operations to get an equivalent expression with no like terms and no parentheses. To simplify the expression $5x + 2 + 3x - 1$, combine the like terms $5x$ and $3x$ and then the numbers.

   $5x + 2 + 3x - 1$
   $= 5x + 3x + 2 - 1$ ← Commutative Property of Addition.
   $= (5 + 3)x + 2 - 1$ ← Distributive Property.
   $= 8x + 2 - 1$ ← Add.
   $= 8x + 1$ ← Subtract.

   Simplify the expression $3a + 2a$. _____

3. Fill in the blanks to simplify the expression $3m^2 + 3 + m^2$. Write the property of operation used for each step.

   $3m^2 + 3 + m^2$

   $= 3m^2 + m^2 + $ ____   ← _____.

   $= 3m^2 + $ ____ $m^2 + $ ____   ← Identity Property of Multiplication.

   $= ($ ____ $+ $ ____ $)m^2 + $ ____   ← _____.

   $= $ _____ $+ $ ____   ← _____.

4. Simplify each expression.

   $6n + 3 + 2n$ _____

   $9q - 9 - q$ _____

On the Back!

5. Combine like terms to write an equivalent expression for $2x + x + x$.

Toss and Talk

Partner Talk

Share your thinking while you work.

Get Started

Get 10 squares in one color and 10 in another color. Get two number cubes. Take turns with another player or team. Talk about math as you play!

At Your Turn

Toss two number cubes. Add the dots. Find your toss below. Follow the directions. Explain your thinking. Cover the answer. If the answer is taken, lose your turn. Have fun!

Toss	Simplify the expression. Explain how you simplified. Find the result.
2	$5 + 3x - 3 + 2x$
3	$2x^2 + 4x^2 - 5$
4	$\frac{3}{4}x - 4 + \frac{1}{4}x$
5	$6x^2 - 4 - 3x^2$
6	$3.5x - 2 + 2.5x$

7	$5x + 10 - 4x - 7$
8	$2x + 5 + x - 4$
9	$2x^2 + 3 - x^2 + 2 + 2x^2$
10	$4.8x + 5 + 1.2x$
11	$\frac{1}{3}x + 3x + 3 + \frac{2}{3}x$
12	$9x + \frac{3}{4} - 5x - \frac{1}{4}$

$3x + 1$	$3x^2 - 4$	$x + 3$	$4x + 3$
$6x - 2$	$x - 4$	$3x + 1$	$6x + 5$
$5x + 2$	$x + 3$	$3x^2 + 5$	$6x + 5$
$3x^2 + 5$	$6x^2 - 5$	$3x^2 - 4$	$4x + \frac{1}{2}$

How to Win

You win if you are the first to get four connected rectangles, like:

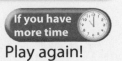

If you have more time

Play again!

Toss and Talk

Get Started 👫 or 👫👫
Get 10 squares in one color and 10 in another color.
Get two number cubes. Take turns with another player or team.
Talk about math as you play!

At Your Turn
Toss two number cubes. Add the dots. Find your toss below.
Follow the directions. Explain your thinking. Cover the answer.
If the answer is taken, lose your turn. Have fun!

Toss	Find another expression that simplifies to the same result. Explain how you simplified.
2	$3x^2 + 10 + 5x^2 - 3$
3	$5x + 20 + 5x - 14 + 5x$
4	$5.3x^2 + 3 - 3.8x^2 + 2.1$
5	$3\frac{1}{4}x - 6 - \frac{3}{4}x + 8$
6	$2.5x^2 + 3 + 0.8x^2 - 1.7$

7	$5.9x + 8.1x + 3 + 3.3$
8	$8x + 5.2 - 3.7x - 2.8$
9	$\frac{2}{3}x + 3 + 5x - \frac{1}{2}$
10	$x^2 + x + 2 + 3x^2 + 4$
11	$3x^2 + 5 + x^2 + 2x - 1$
12	$6x^2 + 3x - 3x^2 - 2x + 3$

$0.3x^2 + 1.3 + 3x^2$	$6.2x + 2.4 - 1.9x$	$2x + 2 + \frac{1}{2}x$	$14x + 3.3 + 3$
$4x^2 + 2x + 4$	$10 + 8x^2 - 3$	$4x^2 + 1.3 - 0.7x^2$	$1.5x^2 + 2.7 + 2.4$
$6x + 8x + 6.3$	$3\frac{1}{3}x + 2\frac{1}{3}x + 2\frac{1}{2}$	$20x + 6 - 5x$	$4x^2 + x + 6$
$x + 3 + 3x^2$	$2x + \frac{1}{2}x + 2$	$6x - \frac{1}{3}x + 2\frac{1}{2}$	$4x + 2.4 + 0.3x$

How to Win
You win if you are the first to get four connected rectangles, like:

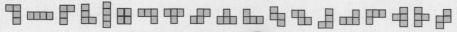

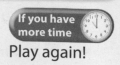
If you have more time
Play again!

Name _____

1. Which is the simplified form of the expression $5a + 12 - a - 12 + 6a$?

Ⓐ $10a - 24$

Ⓑ 10

Ⓒ $12a$

Ⓓ $10a$

2. Which is the simplified form of the expression $6m^2 + 9m - 5m + 4m^2$?

Ⓐ $10m^2 + 4m$

Ⓑ $14m^3$

Ⓒ $14m^2$

Ⓓ $10m^2 + 14m$

Value of Gold Mined in California Counties 1848–1965 (in millions)	
County	**Value**
Nevada	$440
Amador	$200
Tuolumne	$190
Butte	$150

3. What is the value of the gold mined in Tuolumne County?

Ⓐ $190,000,000,000

Ⓑ $190,000,000

Ⓒ $19,000,000

Ⓓ $1,900,000

4. What is the value of $3x - 4$ for $x = 6$?

Ⓐ 32

Ⓑ 14

Ⓒ 8

Ⓓ 6

5. Simplify the expression $7.8x + 9 - 3.5x - 6.2$.

_____

6. Simplify the expression $\frac{5}{6}y^3 + 2y^2 - y^2 - \frac{1}{3}y^3$.

_____

7. What is the value of $2x^2 - 4x + y^3 - 5y$ when $x = 5$ and $y = 3$?

_____

8. How many terms does the expression $\frac{8 \cdot 3}{5} + 6^2 - 10 \div 2$ have?

_____

9. Use the Distributive Property to write an expression that is equivalent to $15\left(\frac{2}{3}r - \frac{4}{5}s\right)$.

_____

10. Write the repeated multiplication expression $5 \times 5 \times 5 \times 5$ as a power.

_____

11. Evaluate $\left(\frac{1}{4}\right)^2$.

_____

D 1·8

6

Name _____

A-Z Vocabulary

1. Two algebraic expressions are **equivalent** if they can be simplified to the same expression. For example, the expressions $3x + 2x + 1$ and $5x + 4 - 3$ are equivalent expressions because they both simplify to $5x + 1$.

Circle the expressions that are equivalent.

$2x + 4$ $6x$ $2(x + 2)$

2. Consider the following expressions.

$10x - 8 - 4x$ $6x + 6 + 2$ $2(3x - 4)$

Simplify $10x - 8 - 4x$. _____

Simplify $6x + 6 + 2$. _____

Simplify $2(3x - 4)$. _____

3. Which of the given expressions in Exercise 2 are equivalent?

_____

4. When $x = 1$, the value of the expression $7x$ is 7 and the value of $4x + 3$ is 7. Explain whether $7x$ and $4x + 3$ are equivalent expressions.

_____

_____

_____

_____

On the Back!

5. Find the values of the following expressions when $z = 1$, $z = 2$, and $z = 3$. Then identify which expressions are equivalent.

$9z - 4 - 3z$ $2(3z - 2)$ $9z - 4z - 3$

Name _____

1. Which expression is equivalent to $33y - 55$?

   (A) $55y - 33$

   (B) $11(3y - 5)$

   (C) $3(11y - 5)$

   (D) $30y + 3y$

2. Which expression is NOT equivalent to the given expression?

   $$14a - 30 + 16a$$

   (A) $30(a - 1)$

   (B) $6(5a - 5)$

   (C) $15(a - 2)$

   (D) $5(6a - 6)$

3. What is the value of the following expression?

   $$6^2 - 4 \cdot 5 + 18 \div 2$$

   (A) 17

   (B) 25

   (C) 89

   (D) 169

4. It costs $35 per day to rent a snowboard at Stratton Mountain in Vermont. Which expressions could represent the cost to rent a snowboard for d days? Select all that apply.

   ☐ $35 + d$

   ☐ $35d$

   ☐ $35 \div d$

   ☐ $d - 35$

   ☐ $35 \times d$

5. Use the Distributive Property to determine whether the two given expressions are equivalent.

   $$32x + 48 \text{ and } 16(2x + 4)$$

   _____

   _____

   _____

   _____

   _____

   _____

6. Complete the table.

y	$y + 3$	$2(y + 1.5)$	$2y + 3$
0			
1			
2			
3			

Which expressions are equivalent?

   _____

   _____

7. How many terms does the expression $9m + \frac{1}{2} \times 3m - 2$ have?

   _____

A-Z Vocabulary

1. A **formula** is a rule that uses symbols to relate two or more quantities. For example, the formula $A = \ell \cdot w$ gives the area of a rectangle, where ℓ is the length and w is the width of the rectangle. You can use the formula to find the area of a rectangle with length 5 feet and width 3 feet.

   $A = \ell \cdot w$
   $A = 5 \cdot 3$
   $A = 15$ square feet

   What is the area of a rectangle with length 6 feet and width 4 feet?

   _____

Paula's car gets 28 miles per gallon. Find the number of miles Paula can travel using 12 gallons of gasoline. Use the formula $d = mg$, where d is distance traveled, m is the miles per gallon, and g is the number of gallons of gasoline used.

2. What value is substituted for m? _____

3. What value is substituted for g? _____

4. Fill in the blanks.

   $d = mg$

   $d = (\_\_\_\_\_)(\_\_\_\_\_)$

   $d = \_\_\_\_\_$

5. How many miles can Paula travel? _____

6. How many miles can Paula travel if she uses 15 gallons of gasoline?

   _____

On the Back!

7. The formula to find the perimeter of a rectangle is $P = 2\ell + 2w$, where ℓ is the length and w is the width of the rectangle. Use the formula to find the perimeter of rectangle *ABDC*.

R 1·9

Name _____

1. The formula for finding the perimeter of a rectangle is $P = 2\ell + 2w$. Use the formula to find the perimeter of this rectangle.

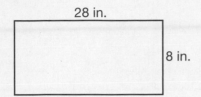

28 in.

8 in.

(A) 1,792 inches

(B) 224 inches

(C) 72 inches

(D) 36 inches

2. The formula $C = \frac{F - 32}{1.8}$ can be used to convert temperatures from degrees Fahrenheit, F, to degrees Celsius, C. Use the formula to convert 77°F to degrees Celsius.

(A) 20°C   (C) 45°C

(B) 25°C   (D) 81°C

3. Which expression is NOT equivalent to the given expression?

$$15x - 40 - 5x$$

(A) $5(3x - 8)$ (C) $2(5x - 20)$

(B) $5(2x - 8)$ (D) $10(x - 4)$

4. Which expression represents 7 less than the product of 11 and a number p?

(A) $7p - 11$ (C) $11p - 7$

(B) $5 - 11p$ (D) $11p + 7$

5. To find the missing angle measure of a triangle, use the formula $a = 180 - (b + c)$, where a, b, and c are the angle measures of the triangle. What is the measure of $\angle P$?

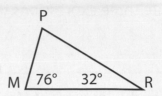

P

M 76°   32°   R

_____

6. The formula $m = \frac{d}{g}$ can be used to calculate gas mileage in miles per gallon, where g is the number of gallons used to travel a distance of d miles. Use the formula to find the gas mileage of Evan's car if it took 11 gallons to travel 308 miles.

_____

7. Complete the table.

x	x + 7	2x + 7	2(x + 3.5)
0			
1			
2			
3			

Which expressions are equivalent?

_____

_____

Name _____

Vocabulary

1. **Equivalent expressions** have the same value regardless of what value is substituted for the same variable in the expressions. Properties of operations can be used to write equivalent expressions. For example, $4(g + 3)$ and $(g + 3)4$ are equivalent expressions by using the Commutative Property of Multiplication.

   Write three expressions that are equivalent to $4(t + 2)$.

   _____

Shawna and Jules work at Mrs. Hill's café. Shawna works 10 hours each week with a $15 weekly bonus, while Jules works 8 hours each week with a $10 weekly bonus. Shawna and Jules earn x dollars per hour. Mrs. Hill uses the algebraic expression $4(10x + 15) + 4(8x + 10)$ to calculate how much she pays them for four weeks of work.

2. Which part of the expression represents the amount Shawna earns in one week?

   _____

3. Which part of the expression represents the amount Jules earns in one week?

   _____

4. Fill in the blanks to write an equivalent expression.

   $4(10x + 15) + 4(8x + 10)$

   = _____ $x +$ _____ $+$ _____ $x +$ _____

   = _____ $x +$ _____

5. How much does Mrs. Hill pay Shawna and Jules for four weeks of work if they both earn $10 per hour?

   _____

On the Back!

6. Marcus is training for a triathlon. He swims at a rate of 3 miles per hour, he runs at a rate of 6.5 miles per hour, and he cycles at a rate of 15 miles per hour. He runs for four times the amount of time that he swims and cycles twice the amount of time he swims. Marcus uses the expression $3 \cdot x + 6.5 \cdot (4x) + 15 \cdot (2x)$ to represent the total miles he travels when he swims for x hours. Which term in Marcus's expression describes the total miles Marcus runs? How far does he travel in total if he swims for half an hour?

Teamwork

Partner Talk
Share your thinking while you work.

Get Started 👫 or 👫👫
Get paper and a pencil.
Put 1 2 3 4 in a bag.

Repeat for Each Round
Choose **a**, **b**, **c**, **d**, **e**, or **f**.
Pick a tile. Pick two tiles if your group has only two students.
Do the jobs listed below in order.
To find your job, find the number that matches the tile you chose.

 1 Write an equivalent expression using the Distributive Property.

 2 Write an equivalent expression using the Commutative Property of Multiplication or Commutative Property of Addition.

 3 Write an expression that is NOT equivalent.

 4 Write two different equivalent expressions. State which properties you used.

a. $4(a + 2) + 4$ b. $3(2b + 1) + 3$

c. $5(2c + 10) + 5c$ d. $7 + 21d + 28$

e. $5e + 10 + 25e$ f. $4f + 8 + 2f + 4$

 **If you have more time**
Choose different values for each variable.
Evaluate your equivalent expressions from Step 4 for the values you chose to verify that your expressions are equivalent.

Center Game ★ 1·10

Teamwork

Partner Talk

Share your thinking while you work.

Get Started

Get paper and a pencil.
Put [1] [2] [3] [4] in a bag.

Repeat for Each Round

Choose **a**, **b**, **c**, **d**, **e**, or **f**.
Pick a tile. Pick two tiles if your group has only two students.
Do the jobs listed below in order.
To find your job, find the number that matches the tile you chose.

---

 1 Write two different equivalent expressions using the Distributive Property and Commutative Property of Addition.

 2 Write two different equivalent expressions using the Distributive Property and the Commutative Property of Multiplication.

 3 Write two different equivalent expressions with at least two terms with variables and no parentheses.

 4 Write two different equivalent expressions using any properties you choose. State which properties you used.

---

a. $8a + 12 + 4a$ b. $32b + 16 + 4b$

c. $8 + 6(c + 4)$ d. $3(2d + 3) + 2(3d + 6)$

e. $4(e + 3) + 8e$ f. $4(3f + 3) + 3(2f - 6)$

 **If you have more time**

Choose several values for each variable.
Evaluate your equivalent expressions for the values you chose to verify that your expressions are equivalent.

Center Game ★★ **1·10**

Name _____

Algebra: Solve Equations and Inequalities

Topic 2 Standards

6.EE.A.4, 6.EE.B.5, 6.EE.B.6, 6.EE.B.7, 6.EE.B.8
See the front of the Student's Edition for complete standards.

Dear Family,

Your child is learning how to write and solve algebraic equations involving addition, subtraction, multiplication, and division, and how to write and solve one-step inequalities. He or she will learn to use variables to represent numbers when solving real-world and mathematical problems. Your child will also learn the properties of equality and use them to solve equations.

Here is an activity that you can do to help your child understand equations and inequalities.

How Much Is That?

Look for ads in newspapers that give prices of groceries, electronics, toys, sporting goods, and other items that are of interest to your child. Use the ads to have your child write an equation. Suppose an ad shows a bicycle on sale for $80. Examples of equations are shown below.

If you save $5 each week, what equation shows how long it would take to save enough money to buy the bike? $5x = 80$, where x represents the number of weeks.

If you already have $25, what equation shows how much more you will need to buy the bicycle? $y + 25 = 80$, where y represents dollars still needed to buy the bicycle.

Help your child solve each of the equations. ($x = 16$ weeks, $y = \$55$)

Then state that you need at least $80 to buy the bicycle. Ask your child to write an inequality to represent this situation. (Let m represent the amount of money a person has if they can buy the bicycle; $m \geq 80$.)

Observe Your Child

Focus on Mathematical Practice 5
Use appropriate tools strategically.

Help your child become proficient with Mathematical Practice 5. A number line is an appropriate tool to use to describe the possible solutions of an inequality. Ask your child to represent the inequality from the activity above on a number line. Ask him or her to explain why the solution arrow points in one direction, and why he or she used an open or closed circle on the number-line graph.

Álgebra: Resolver ecuaciones y desigualdades

Estándares del Tema 2

6.EE.A.4, 6.EE.B.5, 6.EE.B.6, 6.EE.B.7, 6.EE.B.8

Los estándares completos se encuentran en las páginas preliminares del Libro del estudiante.

Estimada familia:

Su niño(a) está aprendiendo a escribir y resolver ecuaciones algebraicas que incluyen suma, resta, multiplicación y división, y a escribir y resolver desigualdades de un paso. Aprenderá a usar variables para representar cantidades cuando resuelva problemas matemáticos y de la vida diaria. Su niño(a) también aprenderá las propiedades de igualdad y a usarlas para resolver ecuaciones.

Pruebe esta actividad con su niño(a) para entender las ecuaciones y las desigualdades.

¿Cuánto es?

Busque anuncios en los periódicos que indiquen precios de comestibles, electrodomésticos, juguetes, ropa deportiva y otros productos que interesen a su niño(a). Use los anuncios para que su niño(a) escriba una ecuación. Suponga que un anuncio muestra una bicicleta a la venta por $80. Se muestran a continuación ejemplos de ecuaciones.

Si ahorras $5 por semana, ¿qué ecuación muestra cuánto tardarás en ahorrar lo suficiente para comprar la bicicleta? $5x = 80$, donde x representa la cantidad de semanas.

Si ya tienes $25, ¿qué ecuación muestra cuánto más necesitarás para comprar la bicicleta? $y + 25 = 80$, donde y representa los dólares que aún necesitas para comprar la bicicleta.

Ayude a su niño(a) a resolver las ecuaciones. ($x = 16$ semanas, $y = 55)

Luego, indique que se necesitan como mínimo $80 para comprar la bicicleta. Pida a su niño(a) que escriba una desigualdad para representar esta situación. (Sea d la cantidad de dinero que una persona tiene si puede comprar la bicicleta; $d \geq 80$.)

Observe a su niño(a)

Enfoque en la Práctica matemática 5
Usar herramientas apropiadas de manera estratégica.

Ayude a su niño(a) a adquirir competencia en la Práctica matemática 5. Una recta numérica es una herramienta apropiada para describir las soluciones posibles para una desigualdad. Pida a su niño(a) que represente la desigualdad de la actividad de arriba sobre una recta numérica. Pídale que explique por qué la flecha de la solución apunta en una dirección y por qué usó un círculo abierto o cerrado sobre la gráfica de la recta numérica.

Name _____

#1 PET Bottles

Did You Know? Many plastic bottles are made out of polyethylene terephthalate, or PET for short. Bottles made out of PET are stamped with the #1 recycling code. After a PET bottle is collected for recycling, it is sorted, inspected, and washed. Then it is chopped up into small flakes and melted. The melted plastic is formed into strands. The strands are then chopped into pellets, which can be used to make new products like clothing, sleeping bags, and park benches.

Items Made with Recycled PET Bottles	
Item	Number of PET Bottles
XL T-shirt	19
Sweater	63
Fiberfill for ski jacket	14
Fiberfill for sleeping bag	114

1. Harper collected 95 plastic water bottles. Use the equation $95 = 19t$ to find the number of XL T-shirts, t, that can be made from the bottles she collected.

   _____

   _____

2. Write an equation to find the number of ski jackets that can be made from 112 PET bottles. Solve the equation.

   _____

   _____

3. **Extension** The students in Cort's class are collecting plastic bottles to recycle. The first week, the class collects 340 bottles. The second week, the class collects 542 bottles. Write and solve an equation to find the number of sweaters, s, that can be made with the bottles the class collected.

   _____

   _____

   6

Name _____

Biodegradable Materials

Did You Know? It can take up to 1 million years for a glass bottle to biodegrade. Man-made materials, especially materials made from fossil fuels, can take centuries to biodegrade. Some plastics never biodegrade. But these materials can be recyclable! By definition, biodegradable material can dissolve quickly into raw materials of the natural environment. Any material that comes from nature, like a leaf or an eggshell, is biodegradable.

Leaves
1–3 Months

Orange Peel
3–6 Months

Aluminum Can
80–200 Years

Plastic 6-Pk Ring
400–500 Years

Plastic Bottle
400–500 Years

Glass Bottle
500 Years-Forever?

1 The length of time, t, it takes a sheet of paper to biodegrade is at least 2 weeks. Write an inequality to represent the time it takes a sheet of paper to biodegrade.

_____

2 A plastic bag takes at least 10 years to biodegrade, but no more than 20 years. Write two inequalities that describe the length of time, b, it takes a plastic bag to biodegrade. Then write two integers that are solutions of both inequalities.

_____

3 **Extension** A foam cup takes 10 times as long as a milk carton takes to biodegrade. The sole of a rubber boot takes 16 times as long as a milk carton takes to biodegrade. The sum of the years it takes for all three items to biodegrade is 135 years. How long does it take for each item to biodegrade? Show your work.

_____

_____

_____

_____

  6

1. Evaluate $3(x + 11)$ for $x = 2$.

Ⓐ 39

Ⓑ 37

Ⓒ 26

Ⓓ 17

2. How would this word phrase be written as an algebraic expression?

6 less than the number r

Ⓐ $6 + r$

Ⓑ $r - 6$

Ⓒ $6 \times r$

Ⓓ $6 - r$

3. What is the value of $n \div 8$ if $n = 128$?

Ⓐ 1,024

Ⓑ 136

Ⓒ 120

Ⓓ 16

4. Matthew has a counter on his website. After 14 months, he had 100,000 hits. What is this number written in exponential form?

Ⓐ 10^6

Ⓑ 10^5

Ⓒ 10^4

Ⓓ 10^3

5. To find a missing angle measure in a triangle, use the formula $a = 180 - (b + c)$, where a, b, and c are the angle measures of the triangle. What is the missing angle measure in the figure?

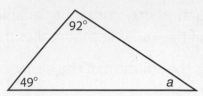

_____

6. Darla is 3 times as old as her sister Julia. Write an algebraic expression for Darla's age. Let x represent Julia's age.

_____

7. Evaluate 8^3.

_____

8. Simplify $5 + 2^3 \times 3 \div 2$.

_____

9. Use the Distributive Property to write an expression equivalent to $4(x + 3)$.

_____

D 2·1

Name _____

🄰🄯 Vocabulary

1. An **equation** is a mathematical sentence that uses an equal sign to show that two expressions are equal. An equation is true when both sides are equal.

   Tell if the equation is true or false.

   The equation $12 - 6.7 = 5.3$ is _____.

2. An equation may contain a variable. A **solution** of an equation is a value of the variable that makes the equation true.

   What is the solution of the equation $8m = 72$? _____

3. Tell if the equation $35 \div r = 5$ is true or false for $r = 7$. _____

   What is the solution of this equation? _____

4. You can determine if a number is a solution of an equation by substituting that number for the variable in the equation.

   Substitute each value in the set for the variable to determine whether it is the solution of the equation $16.6 - t = 11.9$.

   $t = 3.6, 4.4, 4.7, 5.4$

   Try 3.6.
   $16.6 - 3.6 = 13$, so 3.6 is not the solution.

   Try 4.4.
   $16.6 -$ _____ $= 12.2$, so 4.4 _____ the solution.

   Try 4.7. Show your work.

   _____

   Try 5.4. Show your work.

   _____

   The solution of the equation $16.6 - t = 11.9$ is _____.

On the Back!

5. Tell which value of the variable is the solution of the equation.
   $9.4 = k + 5.07$ $\qquad\qquad$ $k = 3.33, 4.33, 4.47, 14.47$

Toss and Talk

Partner Talk
Share your thinking while you work.

Toss	Which value of y makes the equation true? Use mental math.
2	$7y = 21$
3	$y - 18 = 9$
4	$18.2 - y = 8.2$
5	$4y = 20$
6	$11.5 + y = 23.5$

7	$y \div 2 = 15$
8	$4y = 36$
9	$42 = 7y$
10	$y \div 5 = 5$
11	$4y = 16$
12	$y + 7 = 77$

$y = 6$	$y = 3$	$y = 25$	$y = 70$
$y = 12$	$y = 70$	$y = 10$	$y = 12$
$y = 27$	$y = 9$	$y = 6$	$y = 5$
$y = 30$	$y = 5$	$y = 4$	$y = 9$

How to Win

You win if you are the first to get four connected rectangles, like:

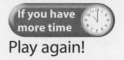
If you have more time
Play again!

Toss and Talk

Share your thinking while you work.

Partner Talk

Get Started
👥 or 👥👥

Get 10 squares in one color and 10 in another color.
Get two number cubes. Take turns with another player or team.
Talk about math as you play!

At Your Turn

Toss two number cubes. Add the dots. Find your toss below. Follow the directions. Explain your thinking. Cover the answer. If the answer is taken, lose your turn. Have fun!

Toss	Use mental math. Find an equation that has this solution. Explain why the equation has this solution.
2	$n = 10$
3	$n = 1$
4	$n = 100$
5	$n = 6$
6	$n = 0$

7	$n = 20$
8	$n = 12$
9	$n = 2$
10	$n = 30$
11	$n = 8$
12	$n = 5$

$7n = 35$	$3n = 60$	$12 - n = 0$	$9n = 0$
$n \div 2 = 1$	$4n = 24$	$5n = 60$	$16.8 - n = 11.8$
$n \div 1 = 1$	$9n = 18$	$6n = 36$	$n - 50 = 50$
$150n = 0$	$5n = 40$	$n - 3 = 27$	$8n = 80$

How to Win

You win if you are the first to get four connected rectangles, like:

If you have more time
Play again!

In **1** and **2**, choose the value of the variable that makes the equation true.

1. $63 = 9t$ $\qquad$ $t = 3, 5, 7$

$\textcircled{A}$ 3

$\textcircled{B}$ 5

$\textcircled{C}$ 7

$\textcircled{D}$ No solution is given in the set of values.

2. $9.8 + c = 16.3$ $\qquad$ $c = 6.4, 7.5, 8.6$

$\textcircled{A}$ 6.4

$\textcircled{B}$ 7.5

$\textcircled{C}$ 8.6

$\textcircled{D}$ No solution is given in the set of values.

3. Which is equivalent to the expression $8p + 12p^2 - 11p^2 + p$?

$\textcircled{A}$ $p^2 + 9p$

$\textcircled{B}$ $20p^2 - 10p$

$\textcircled{C}$ $10p^2$

$\textcircled{D}$ $10p^3$

4. Which expression is NOT equivalent to $30x - 12 - 6x$? Select all that apply.

$\square$ $3(8x - 4)$

$\square$ $4(6x - 2)$

$\square$ $6(4x - 2)$

$\square$ $12(2x - 1)$

$\square$ $24(x - 2)$

5. Alyssa says that $n = 6$ is the solution of the equation $12n = 84$. How can you check whether she is correct?

_____

_____

_____

_____

6. What is the coefficient of y in the expression $\frac{1}{2}x + \frac{3}{4}y - 10$?

_____

7. Evaluate each expression for each value of x to complete the table.

x	$x + 7.5$	$3x + 7.5$	$3(x + 2.5)$
0			
1			
2			
3			

Which expressions are equivalent?

_____

_____

8. Write an expression for 7 divided by a number n.

_____

Name _____

A-Z Vocabulary

1. The **Addition Property of Equality** states that when you add the same amount to both sides of an equation, the two sides of the equation stay equal.

   $22 - 7 = 15$, so $(22 - 7) + 10 = 15 +$ _____.

2. The **Subtraction Property of Equality** states that when you subtract the same amount from both sides of an equation, the two sides of the equation stay equal.

   $25 + 12 = 37$, so $(25 + 12) - 9 = 37 -$ _____.

3. The **Multiplication Property of Equality** states that when you multiply both sides of an equation by the same amount, the two sides of the equation stay equal.

   $18 - 4 = 14$, so $(18 - 4) \times 3 = 14 \times$ _____.

4. The **Division Property of Equality** states that when you divide both sides of an equation by the same non-zero amount, the two sides of the equation stay equal.

   $8 + 6 = 14$, so $(8 + 6) \div 7 = 14 \div$ _____.

Complete the statements. Then write the property of equality that is illustrated by the statement.

5. If $\frac{y}{8} = 4$, then $\frac{y}{8} \cdot 8 = 4 \cdot$ _____.   _____

6. If $4 + x = 34$, then $4 + x - 4 = 34 -$ _____.   _____

7. If $3.5m = 14$, then $3.5m \div 3.5 = 14 \div$ _____.   _____

8. If $g - 6 = 10$, then $g - 6 + 6 = 10 +$ _____.   _____

On the Back!

9. Tell which property of equality was used.

   $6z = 90$
   $6z \div 6 = 90 \div 6$

Name _____

1. Which property is shown below?
$4w = 40$, so $4w \div 4 = 40 \div 4$.

  Ⓐ Addition Property of Equality

  Ⓑ Subtraction Property of Equality

  Ⓒ Multiplication Property of Equality

  Ⓓ Division Property of Equality

2. Evaluate the expression
$7 + 3^2 \div 9$.

  Ⓐ 11.5

  Ⓑ 10

  Ⓒ 8

  Ⓓ 6.5

3. Evaluate the expression for $t = 7$.
$8 + (t - 3) \div 4$

  Ⓐ 3

  Ⓑ 6

  Ⓒ 9

  Ⓓ 12

4. Which value of b makes the equation
$b \div 6 = 18$ true?

  Ⓐ $b = 3$

  Ⓑ $b = 9$

  Ⓒ $b = 96$

  Ⓓ $b = 108$

5. Which property of equality was used?

$$79 = 55 + 2r$$
$$79 - 55 = (55 + 2r) - 55$$

_____

6. If $\frac{n}{12} = 20$, does $\left(\frac{n}{12}\right) \cdot 12 = 20 \cdot 20$?
Explain.

_____

_____

_____

_____

7. Use the formula $A = \ell \cdot w$, where ℓ
is a rectangle's length and w is its
width, to find the area, A, of the
rectangle below.

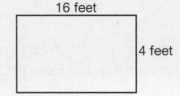

16 feet

4 feet

_____

8. Evaluate the algebraic expression
$(5 + x^2) \div 2$ for $x = 7$.

_____

D 2·3

Name _____

⚫Vocabulary

1. Operations that *undo* each other have an **inverse relationship.**

   Addition and _____ have an inverse relationship.

   Multiplication and _____ have an inverse relationship.

In 2–4, complete the solution as you fill in the blanks.

2. What operation is being used in the equation? $x + 15 = 22$

   _____

3. What operation has an inverse relationship to the $x + 15 - \square = 22 - \square$
   operation identified in Exercise 2?

                                                              $x = \square$

   _____

4. To solve the equation, subtract _____ from both sides of the equation.

In 5–7, complete the solution as you fill in the blanks.

5. What operation is being used in the equation? $y - 11 = 20$

   _____

6. What operation has an inverse relationship to the $y - 11 + \square = 20 + \square$
   operation identified in Exercise 5?

                                                              $y = \square$

   _____

7. To solve the equation, add _____ to both sides of the equation.

On the Back!

8. Write an equation and solve for the variable.

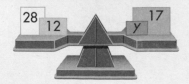

Think Together

Partner Talk

Share your thinking while you work.

Get Started or

Put 1 2 3 4 in a bag. Get paper and a pencil.

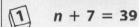

For Each Round

Choose A, B, C, D, E, or F.
Pick a tile. Pick two tiles if your group has only two students.
Solve the equation next to your number.
Discuss: Which three equations can be solved using the same Property of Equality? Why?
Decide: Is each solution correct? How can you check?

A Solve for the variable.

1. $n + 7 = 39$
2. $r + 16 = 44$
3. $a - 8 = 17$
4. $x + 15 = 65$

B Solve for the variable.

1. $c - 8 = 12$
2. $r - 15 = 16$
3. $b + 9 = 37$
4. $x - 5 = 26$

C Solve for the variable.

1. $w + 9 = 32$
2. $x - 23 = 51$
3. $y - 2.5 = 15$
4. $z - 25 = 150$

D Solve for the variable.

1. $x - 7.6 = 15.2$
2. $z + 26 = 47$
3. $r + 13.2 = 15$
4. $a + 52 = 70$

E Solve for the variable.

1. $18 = x + 4$
2. $36 = c + 9$
3. $y - 34 = 72$
4. $w + 52 = 71$

F Solve for the variable.

1. $15 = r - 29$
2. $s - 62 = 57$
3. $49 = x + 37$
4. $81 = t - 32$

If you have more time

Make up a "Think Together" set of equations like these.
Challenge your classmates to think together to solve your equations.

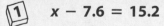

Center Game ★ 2-3

Think Together

Partner Talk
Share your thinking while you work.

 **Get Started** or

Put $\boxed{1}$ $\boxed{2}$ $\boxed{3}$ $\boxed{4}$ in a bag. Get paper and a pencil.

 For Each Round

Choose A, B, C, D, E, or **F.**
Pick a tile. Pick two tiles if your group has only two students.
Solve the equation next to your number.
Explain: How do you get the variable alone?
Decide: Which equation is solved in a different way from the other three? Why?

A Solve for the variable.

$\boxed{1}$ $74 = x - 15$

$\boxed{2}$ $13 + c = 91$

$\boxed{3}$ $48 = 17 + r$

$\boxed{4}$ $87 = y + 29$

B Solve for the variable.

$\boxed{1}$ $15 + b = 42$

$\boxed{2}$ $77 = 14 + k$

$\boxed{3}$ $24 = x - 90$

$\boxed{4}$ $92 + f = 118$

C Solve for the variable.

$\boxed{1}$ $59 = r - 15$

$\boxed{2}$ $75 = 13 + y$

$\boxed{3}$ $m - 27 = 61$

$\boxed{4}$ $69 = q - 14$

D Solve for the variable.

$\boxed{1}$ $t - 27 = 78$

$\boxed{2}$ $51 = r - 19$

$\boxed{3}$ $34 = x - 92$

$\boxed{4}$ $32 + y = 47$

E Solve for the variable.

$\boxed{1}$ $63 + c = 122$

$\boxed{2}$ $m - 46 = 51$

$\boxed{3}$ $100 = x + 17$

$\boxed{4}$ $82 = 15 + t$

F Solve for the variable.

$\boxed{1}$ $5 + y = 17$

$\boxed{2}$ $103 = d + 75.2$

$\boxed{3}$ $42 + k = 50.7$

$\boxed{4}$ $37.1 = j - 14.3$

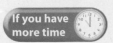 **If you have more time**

Make up a "Think Together" set of equations like these.
Challenge your classmates to think together to solve your equations.

Center Game ★★ **2·3**

1. Which of the following explains how to get the variable alone on one side of the equation?
   $n - 24 = 17$

   Ⓐ Add 17 to both sides.

   Ⓑ Subtract 17 from both sides.

   Ⓒ Add 24 to both sides.

   Ⓓ Subtract 24 from both sides.

2. Which equations have $z = 42$ as the solution? Select all that apply.

   ☐ $28 + z = 70$

   ☐ $50 - z = 6$

   ☐ $z + 81 = 123$

   ☐ $z - 6 = 38$

   ☐ $z - 40 = 2$

3. Which expression describes 4 more than twice a number of airplanes? Let a represent the number of airplanes.

   Ⓐ $2a + 4$

   Ⓑ $2(a + 4)$

   Ⓒ $a(2 + 4)$

   Ⓓ $4a + 2$

4. Which of the following is equivalent to $8 \times 8 \times 8 \times 8 \times 8$?

   Ⓐ 8×5

   Ⓑ 8^5

   Ⓒ 5^8

   Ⓓ $4,096$

5. Explain how to get the variable alone on one side of the equation.
   $75 = 48 + y$

   _____

   _____

6. Solve the equation. Show your work.
   $$m - 253 = 459$$

   _____

   _____

7. How many terms does the expression $7c - 8d + 2 \div e$ have?

   _____

Dan has 18 movie posters in his collection. After he buys more posters, he has 23 in his collection. How many posters did Dan buy?

8. Let p represent the number of posters that Dan bought. Write an equation to represent the problem.

   _____

9. Solve the equation and answer the question.

   _____

   _____

D 2·4

Name _____

Vocabulary

1. Two operations have an **inverse relationship** if they *undo* each other.

   Addition and _____ have an inverse relationship.

   $n + 3 - 3 = n$ $t - 8 + _____ = t$

   Multiplication and _____ have an inverse relationship.

   $4d \div 4 = _____$ $g \div 7 \cdot _____ = g$

2. Solve the equation $9p = 54$.

   $9p = 54$

   $9p \div 9 = 54 \div _____$

   $p = _____$

   Which property of equality did you use to solve the equation?

   _____

3. Solve the equation $x \div 4 = 30$.

   $x \div 4 = 30$

   $x \div 4 \cdot _____ = 30 \cdot _____$

   $x = _____$

   Which property of equality did you use to solve the equation?

   _____

4. Maria solved the equation $7d = 56$ and found the solution $d = 8$.

   She can check her solution by substituting _____ for d in
   the original equation.

   $7d = 56$

   $7 \cdot _____ = _____$

   $_____ = _____$ It checks.

On the Back!

5. Explain how to solve the equation $8 = \frac{p}{12}$.

R 2·4

Name _____

1. Dan owns 5 times as many sports cards as Pedro. If Dan owns 500 cards, which equation could you use to find the number of sports cards that Pedro owns, n?

   Ⓐ $5n = 500$

   Ⓑ $\frac{5}{n} = 500$

   Ⓒ $5 + n = 500$

   Ⓓ $5 - n = 500$

2. Which of the following explains how to get the variable alone?
   $\frac{p}{5} = 9$

   Ⓐ Multiply both sides by 9.

   Ⓑ Add 5 to both sides.

   Ⓒ Divide both sides by 5.

   Ⓓ Multiply both sides by 5.

3. Mikaela counted 2 more turtle nests on a beach than Diego counted. If Mikaela counted 38 turtle nests, which equation could you use to find the number of turtle nests Diego counted, x?

   Ⓐ $2x = 38$

   Ⓑ $x \div 2 = 38$

   Ⓒ $x - 2 = 38$

   Ⓓ $x + 2 = 38$

4. Solve the equation $6x = 72$.

   Ⓐ $x = 8$ Ⓒ $x = 12$

   Ⓑ $x = 10$ Ⓓ $x = 66$

In **5** and **6**, explain how to get the variable alone in each equation.

5. $84 + c = 111$

   _____

   _____

6. $y \div 6 = 7$

   _____

   _____

7. Use the order of operations to evaluate the expression for $x = 3$.
   $5x + (18 - 2x) + 16 \div 4 \times 2^3$

   _____

8. Write and solve an equation to answer this question.

   Kelly collected 84 cans for recycling. That is 3 times as many cans as her sister collected. How many cans did her sister collect?

   _____

   _____

   _____

   _____

   _____

D 2·5

Name _____

A-Z Vocabulary

1. Two numbers are **reciprocals** if their product is 1.

   $\frac{4}{5}$ and $\frac{5}{4}$ are reciprocals because $\frac{4}{5} \times \frac{5}{4} =$ _____.

   $\frac{9}{7}$ and _____ are reciprocals because $\frac{9}{7} \times$ _____ $= 1$.

2. You can use inverse relationships of operations and the properties of equality to solve equations with fractions and mixed numbers.

   To solve $3\frac{3}{4} + r = 5\frac{3}{8}$, use the _____ Property of Equality.

   $$3\frac{3}{4} + r = 5\frac{3}{8}$$

   $$3\frac{3}{4} + r - 3\frac{3}{4} = 5\frac{3}{8} - \underline{\hspace{1cm}}$$

   $$r = \underline{\hspace{1cm}}$$

3. To solve multiplication equations involving fractions, you can multiply both sides by the reciprocal of the fraction.

   $\frac{2}{5}w = 40$

   What is the reciprocal of $\frac{2}{5}$? _____

   _____ $\cdot \frac{2}{5}w =$ _____ $\cdot 40$

   $$w = \underline{\hspace{1cm}}$$

4. How would you solve each equation?

   $r - 5\frac{2}{3} = 8\frac{5}{6}$ _____

   $\frac{v}{9} = 10\frac{1}{3}$ _____

On the Back!

5. Solve the equation.

   $t + \frac{4}{5} = 8\frac{1}{2}$

Toss and Talk

Get Started 👫 or 👫👫

Get 10 squares in one color and 10 in another color.
Get two number cubes. Take turns with another player or team.
Talk about math as you play!

At Your Turn

Toss two number cubes. Add the dots. Find your toss below.
Follow the directions. Explain your thinking. Cover the answer.
If the answer is taken, lose your turn. Have fun!

Toss	Look at the equation. Tell which operation you will use to solve the equation. Then solve.
2	$x - 1\frac{5}{8} = 2\frac{1}{4}$
3	$4\frac{5}{9} = x + 2\frac{1}{3}$
4	$\frac{2}{9}x = 3$
5	$4\frac{3}{8} - 1\frac{3}{4} = x$
6	$x - 1\frac{1}{3} = 2\frac{3}{4}$

7	$\frac{x}{4} = 7$
8	$4\frac{2}{5} - 2\frac{1}{2} = x$
9	$\frac{5}{6}x = 5$
10	$x - 3\frac{1}{4} = 2\frac{1}{2}$
11	$x - 2\frac{7}{10} = 1\frac{1}{5}$
12	$\frac{x}{5} = \frac{1}{2}$

$x = 2\frac{5}{8}$	$x = 13\frac{1}{2}$	$x = 2\frac{1}{2}$	$x = 28$
$x = 5\frac{3}{4}$	$x = 1\frac{9}{10}$	$x = 4\frac{1}{12}$	$x = 3\frac{7}{8}$
$x = 2\frac{2}{9}$	$x = 28$	$x = 6$	$x = 3\frac{9}{10}$
$x = 4\frac{1}{12}$	$x = 6$	$x = 2\frac{5}{8}$	$x = 1\frac{9}{10}$

How to Win

You win if you are the first to get four connected rectangles, like:

If you have more time
Play again!

Toss and Talk

Partner Talk
Share your thinking while you work.

Get Started  Get 10 squares in one color and 10 in another color. Get two number cubes. Take turns with another player or team. Talk about math as you play!

At Your Turn Toss two number cubes. Add the dots. Find your toss below. Follow the directions. Explain your thinking. Cover the answer. If the answer is taken, lose your turn. Have fun!

Toss	Look at the equation. Tell which operation you will use to solve the equation. Then solve.
2	$4\frac{1}{3} = x + 2\frac{5}{6}$
3	$2\frac{3}{4} = x - 1\frac{2}{3}$
4	$2\frac{7}{12}x = 2\frac{3}{14}$
5	$\frac{7}{10} = 7x$
6	$7\frac{1}{4} = \frac{x}{6}$

7	$\frac{7}{4}x = 21$
8	$x + \frac{1}{2} = 4\frac{2}{5}$
9	$3\frac{5}{12}x = 4\frac{1}{10}$
10	$\frac{x}{8} = 5\frac{1}{8}$
11	$x - 4\frac{1}{2} = 1\frac{3}{5}$
12	$x + 2\frac{3}{5} = 4\frac{7}{10}$

$x = \frac{1}{10}$	$x = 6\frac{1}{10}$	$x = 1\frac{1}{5}$	$x = 43\frac{1}{2}$
$x = 41$	$x = 3\frac{9}{10}$	$x = 12$	$x = 1\frac{1}{2}$
$x = 2\frac{1}{10}$	$x = 43\frac{1}{2}$	$x = 1\frac{1}{5}$	$x = \frac{6}{7}$
$x = 12$	$x = \frac{1}{10}$	$x = 4\frac{5}{12}$	$x = 3\frac{9}{10}$

How to Win You win if you are the first to get four connected rectangles, like:

If you have more time
Play again!

Center Game ★★ 2·5

1. Which of the following explains how to get the variable alone on one side of the equation?

   $\frac{5}{6}y = 35$

   (A) Subtract $\frac{5}{6}$ from both sides.

   (B) Multiply both sides by $\frac{5}{6}$.

   (C) Multiply both sides by $\frac{6}{5}$.

   (D) Divide both sides by $\frac{6}{5}$.

2. Which value of g makes the following equation true?

   $g - 1\frac{5}{6} = \frac{1}{3}$

   (A) $g = 2\frac{1}{6}$ (C) $g = 1\frac{1}{3}$

   (B) $g = 1\frac{1}{2}$ (D) $g = \frac{2}{3}$

3. Steve earned $78, which he plans to spend on a $129 skateboard. Which equation could you use to find how much more money, m, Steve needs to buy the skateboard?

   (A) $78 + m = 129$

   (B) $129 + 78 = m$

   (C) $m + 129 = 78$

   (D) $87 - m = 129$

4. Which algebraic expression represents 4 more than twice the number of p pears?

   (A) $p + 4$

   (B) $4 - 2p$

   (C) $8p$

   (D) $2p + 4$

5. Solve the equation $\frac{3}{4} + b = 3$.

   _____

6. Evaluate $2 + \frac{4}{5}n$ for $n = \frac{1}{4}$.

   _____

7. Use the formula $V = \ell wh$, where ℓ is the length, w is the width, and h is the height of the prism to find the volume, V, of the rectangular prism below.

   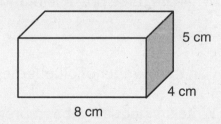

   5 cm

   4 cm

   8 cm

   _____

8. Evaluate $4x - 8$ for $x = 3$ and for $x = 4$.

   _____

Name _____

Vocabulary

1. A mathematical sentence that contains < (less than), > (greater than), ≤ (less than or equal to), ≥ (greater than or equal to), or ≠ (not equal to) is an **inequality.**

   Use an inequality symbol to complete each statement.

   A number, n, is less than 50. n ◯ 50

   A number, p, is greater than 37. p ◯ 37

   Erin's age, e, is greater than or equal to 12. e ◯ 12

   Gabriel's age, g, is less than or equal to 15. g ◯ 15

   Ramon's test score, r, is not 85. r ◯ 85

Morgan ate at least 20 blueberries. Let $m =$ the number of blueberries that Morgan ate.

2. What are three possible numbers of blueberries that Morgan ate?

   _____

3. Can the number of blueberries that Morgan ate be exactly 20? _____

4. Write an inequality that represents the possible number of blueberries that Morgan ate.

   _____

Kayla is at most 56 inches tall. Let $k =$ Kayla's height.

5. What are three possible heights for Kayla?

   _____

6. Can Kayla's height be exactly 56 inches? _____

7. Write an inequality that represents Kayla's possible heights. _____

On the Back!

8. Write an inequality for the situation.

   The number of teachers, t, at Riverside Middle School is greater than 35.

Name _____

1. Which inequality describes the situation?
   The distance, d, that Jason needs to drive on Monday is at least 235 miles.

   Ⓐ $d > 235$

   Ⓑ $d < 235$

   Ⓒ $d \geq 235$

   Ⓓ $d \leq 235$

2. How would you get the variable alone in the equation $4y = 3$?

   Ⓐ Divide both sides of the equation by 4.

   Ⓑ Add 4 to both sides of the equation.

   Ⓒ Multiply both sides of the equation by 4.

   Ⓓ Subtract 3 from both sides of the equation.

3. The formula for the volume of a cube is $V = s^3$, where s is the length of an edge. Which represents the volume of the cube below? Select all that apply.

   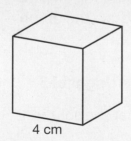

   4 cm

   ☐ $(4 \times 4 \times 4 \times 4)$ cm^3

   ☐ 4 cm $\times$ 4 cm $\times$ 4 cm

   ☐ 12 cm^3

   ☐ 16 cm^3

   ☐ 64 cm^3

In **4** and **5**, write an inequality for each situation.

4. Martin's math test score, m, was greater than 80.

   _____

5. The instructions for a motorized toy car say that the weight, w, of a person using it should be no more than 120 pounds.

   _____

6. Evaluate the expression $5m + 2(m + 8) + 3$ for $m = 2$.

   _____

7. Evaluate the expression for $x = 2$.

   $5x - 3 + 4(x^2) - 13 + 6x - 12$

   _____

8. Solve the equation $p + \frac{5}{8} = \frac{15}{16}$.

   _____

D 2·7

Name _____

A-Z Vocabulary

1. A **solution of an inequality** is a value for the variable that makes the inequality true. A number line can be used to show the solutions of an inequality.

   $x < 2$

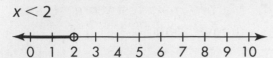

   What is one possible solution for the inequality $x < 2$? _____

2. An inequality can have **infinitely many** solutions, which means an unlimited number of solutions.

3. Write "is" or "is not" in each blank to explain whether the number is a solution to the inequality $d > -2$.

   3 _____ a solution because 3 _____ greater than -2.

   -2 _____ a solution because -2 _____ greater than -2.

4. Circle the correct term and fill in each blank to complete the steps to graphing the solutions of the inequality $d > -2$. Then draw the graph.

   Step 1 Draw a(n) open/closed circle at _____.

   Step 2 Because $d > -2$, shade all of the values to the left/right of -2.

   Step 3 Draw an arrow on the number line to show that the solutions go on forever.

   ```
   ←+—+—+—+—+—+—+—+—+—+—+→
    -5 -4 -3 -2 -1  0  1  2  3  4  5
   ```

5. Circle the correct term and fill in each blank to complete the steps to graphing the solutions of the inequality $y \leq 3$. Then draw the graph.

   Step 1 Draw a(n) open/closed circle at _____.

   Step 2 Because $y \leq 3$, shade all of the values to the left/right of 3.

   Step 3 Draw an arrow on the number line to show that the solutions go on forever.

   ```
   ←+—+—+—+—+—+—+—+—+—+—+→
    -5 -4 -3 -2 -1  0  1  2  3  4  5
   ```

On the Back!

6. Write the inequality that the graph represents.

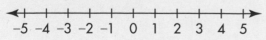

   ```
   ←+—+—+—+—+—+—+—+—+—+—+→
    -5 -4 -3 -2 -1  0  1  2  3  4  5
   ```

Display the Digits

Partner Talk
Share your thinking while you work.

Get Started
👤 or 👥

Pick a tile. Find the graph next to that number. Find the inequality that has the solutions shown on the graph. Explain your choice. Place your tile on the inequality. Display each 0–9 tile exactly once. If you have a partner, take turns.

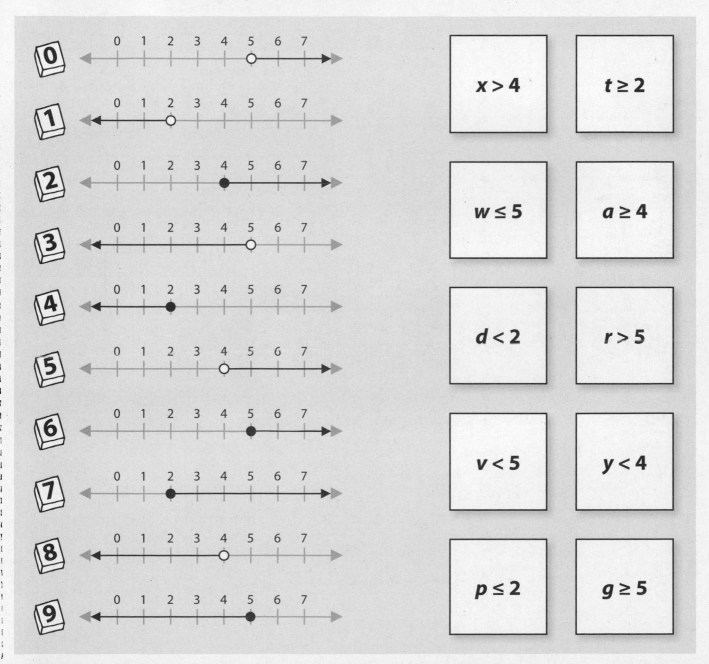

|0| 0 1 2 3 4 5 6 7 (open circle at 5, ray left)

|1| 0 1 2 3 4 5 6 7 (open circle at 2, ray left)

|2| 0 1 2 3 4 5 6 7 (closed circle at 4, ray right)

|3| 0 1 2 3 4 5 6 7 (open circle at 5, ray left)

|4| 0 1 2 3 4 5 6 7 (closed circle at 2, ray left)

|5| 0 1 2 3 4 5 6 7 (open circle at 4, ray right)

|6| 0 1 2 3 4 5 6 7 (closed circle at 5, ray right)

|7| 0 1 2 3 4 5 6 7 (closed circle at 2, ray right)

|8| 0 1 2 3 4 5 6 7 (open circle at 4, ray left)

|9| 0 1 2 3 4 5 6 7 (closed circle at 5, ray left)

$x > 4$	$t \geq 2$
$w \leq 5$	$a \geq 4$
$d < 2$	$r > 5$
$v < 5$	$y < 4$
$p \leq 2$	$g \geq 5$

If you have more time
Make up an inequality. Ask your partner to describe the graph that shows the solutions for your inequality.

Center Game ★ 2-7

Display the Digits

Display the Digits

Get Started
👤 or 👥

Pick a tile. Find the graph next to that number. Find the inequality that has the solutions shown on the graph. Explain your choice. Place your tile on the inequality. Display each 0–9 tile exactly once. If you have a partner, take turns.

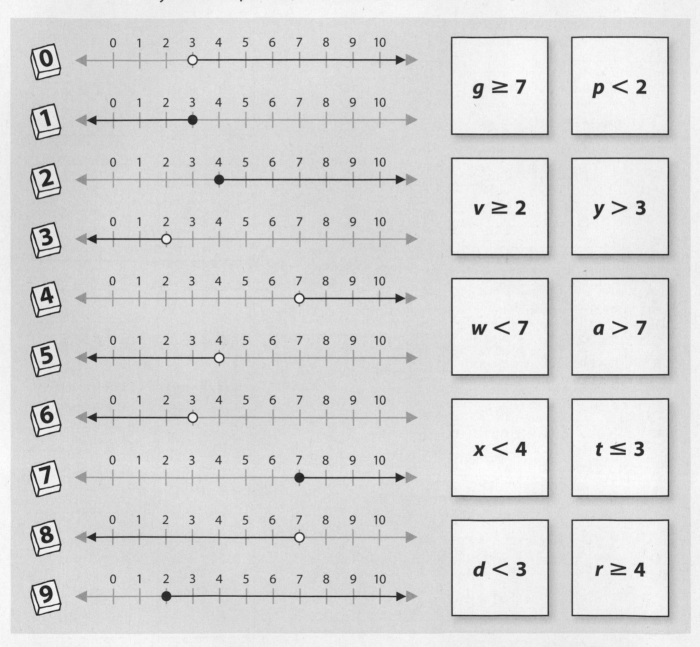

$g \geq 7$	$p < 2$
$v \geq 2$	$y > 3$
$w < 7$	$a > 7$
$x < 4$	$t \leq 3$
$d < 3$	$r \geq 4$

If you have more time

Make up an inequality. Ask your partner to describe the graph that shows the solutions for your inequality.

Center Game ★★ (2·7)

Name _____

1. Which inequality does the graph represent?

Ⓐ $x < 6$

Ⓑ $x \leq 6$

Ⓒ $x > 6$

Ⓓ $x \geq 6$

2. Which of the following lists three solutions of the inequality?

$$y \geq 6.99$$

Ⓐ 4, 5, 6

Ⓑ 6, 7, 8

Ⓒ 7, 8, 9

Ⓓ 6, 8, 10

3. A charity collected $40 for each mile Carlos ran in a race. If the charity received $400, which equation could you use to find the number of miles, m, Carlos ran in that race?

Ⓐ $m + 40 = 400$

Ⓑ $40 \times 400 = m$

Ⓒ $40m = 400$

Ⓓ $40 \div m = 400$

4. Which is the value of the expression $x(9 + x) - 4$ if $x = 8$?

Ⓐ 13

Ⓑ 69

Ⓒ 132

Ⓓ 248

5. Write an inequality using the variable x that can be represented by the graph below.

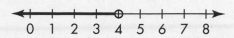

_____

6. Graph the inequality on the number line.

$$y \geq 3$$

< |0 |1 |2 |3 |4 |5 |6 |7 |8 | >

7. Solve the equation.

$$\frac{7}{10}t = 28$$

_____

8. Julia made $35 walking a neighbor's dog for 5 days. If she made the same amount each day she walked the dog, how much did she make each day? Let d represent the amount, in dollars, Julia made each day. Write an equation and use it to solve the problem.

_____

_____

_____

_____

D 2-8

1. To **persevere** means that you keep trying even though the problem may be difficult.

    A synonym for persevere is _____.

The perimeter of parallelogram *ABCD* is 54 inches. The shorter sides of *ABCD* are half as long as the longer sides. What are the side lengths of *ABCD*?

2. Make sense of the problem. What do you know?

    _____

    _____

3. Make sense of the problem. What do you need to find?

    _____

4. What is your plan to solve the problem?

    _____

    _____

5. Solve the problem.

On the Back!

6. Dan ran five days last week. On Tuesday, he ran twice as far as on Monday. On Wednesday, he ran the same distance as on Monday. On Thursday and Friday, he ran half the distance he ran on Monday. If Dan ran a total of 15 miles last week, how far did he run each day?

Name _____

Rational Numbers

Topic 3 Standards

6.NS.C.5, 6.NS.C.6, 6.NS.C.6a, 6.NS.C.6c, 6.NS.C.7a, 6.NS.C.7b, 6.NS.C.7c, 6.NS.C.7d
See the front of the Student's Edition for complete standards.

Dear Family,

   Your child is learning to use integers and other rational numbers to solve problems. A part of this is learning the meanings of integers and how to use them to describe quantities that have opposite directions or values. He or she is also learning how to compare and order these numbers.

   You can help your child understand the concept of negative integers by playing the following game.

What Integer Am I?

Draw a number line on a large sheet of paper.

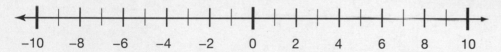

Step 1 Player 1 places a token on any number on the number line. Positive numbers, negative numbers, and zero are all fair game.

Step 2 Player 2 says, "What is my name?" "What is my opposite?" and "How many units am I away from 0?"

Step 3 Player 1 then gives the name of the integer, its opposite, and tells its distance from 0.

Step 4 Trade roles and play again.

Alternate Gameplay: Draw a number line that shows halves and whole numbers from −5 to 5. Place tokens at any location on the number line to talk about positive and negative fractions and decimals.

Observe Your Child

Focus on Mathematical Practice 5
Use appropriate tools strategically.

Help your child become proficient with Mathematical Practice 5. After drawing the number line for the activity above, ask your child where he or she might have seen or used a number line before. Suggest a thermometer or football field if your child has trouble coming up with an idea.

Números racionales

Estándares del Tema 3

6.SN.C.5, 6.SN.C.6, 6.SN.C.6a, 6.SN.C.6c, 6.SN.C.7a, 6.SN.C.7b, 6.SN.C.7c, 6.SN.C.7d
Los estándares completos se encuentran en las páginas preliminares del Libro del estudiante.

Estimada familia:

Su niño(a) está aprendiendo a usar enteros y otros números racionales para resolver problemas. Una parte del aprendizaje consiste en conocer lo que significan los números enteros y cómo usarlos para describir cantidades que tienen sentidos o valores opuestos. También aprenderá a comparar y ordenar estos números.

Puede ayudar a que su niño(a) comprenda el concepto de enteros negativos con el siguiente juego.

¿Qué entero soy?

Dibuje una recta numérica sobre una hoja grande de papel.

Paso 1 El Jugador 1 coloca una ficha sobre cualquier número de la recta numérica. Puede ser sobre números positivos, sobre números negativos o sobre el cero mismo.

Paso 2 El Jugador 2 pregunta "¿cuál es mi nombre?", "¿cuál es mi opuesto?" y "¿a cuántas unidades estoy del 0?".

Paso 3 El Jugador 1, entonces, indica el nombre del número entero, su opuesto, e indica su distancia del 0.

Paso 4 Intercambien roles y vuelvan a jugar.

Modo de juego alternativo: Dibuje una recta numérica que muestre mitades y números enteros del −5 al 5. Coloca las fichas en cualquier lugar sobre la recta numérica para conversar sobre fracciones positivas y negativas y números decimales.

Observe a su niño(a)

Enfoque en la Práctica matemática 5
Usar herramientas apropiadas de manera estratégica.

Ayude a su niño(a) a adquirir competencia en la Práctica matemática 5. Luego de dibujar la recta numérica para la actividad de arriba, pregunte a su niño(a) dónde observó o usó una recta numérica antes. Recuerde un termómetro o un campo de fútbol si su niño(a) tiene problemas en encontrar una respuesta.

Name _____

The Second Highest Mountain

> **Did You Know?** Mount Everest is well
> known as the highest mountain in the
> world, but did you know that a mountain
> in Asia called K2 is the second highest? It's
> slightly shorter than Mount Everest, but K2
> has such severe snowstorms that it is even
> more difficult to climb.

1 Mount Everest is about $\frac{1}{4}$ kilometer taller than K2. Plot $\frac{1}{4}$ on the
number line.

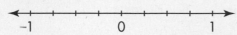

2 The temperature at which water boils at sea level is 100°C.
K2 is so tall that water boils at 72.6°C. On Mount Everest, water
boils at 72.0°C, an even lower temperature. If you subtract the
temperature at which water boils on K2 from the temperature at
which water boils on Mount Everest, the result is −0.6 degrees.
Plot −0.6 on the number line.

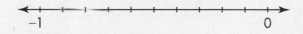

3 **Represent** Draw and label a thermometer that shows −26°C,
a possible temperature at base camp on K2 in the winter.

4 **Extension** The table at the right shows possible temperatures
on K2 at different times throughout the year. Draw a number line.
Plot and label each temperature.

Temperature (° Celsius)
−35.5
−31.0
−28.0
−25.5

Name _____

Mount McKinley

> **Did You Know?** The tallest mountain in the United States is Mount McKinley in Alaska. Its native name is Denali, which means "The High One." Its summit is over 6 kilometers high. It is known for its extremely cold weather. At its peak, the temperature can dip as low as −75°F.

1 A hiker summited Mount McKinley and measured the temperature at its peak at −52°F. By the time the hiker reached the base of the mountain, the temperature had risen 60 degrees. What was the temperature at the base of Mount McKinley?

2 **Represent** A meteorologist measures the temperature at the base of Mount McKinley as 3°F. The table at the right shows how the temperature changes over the next three days. What is the temperature on Day 4? Show your work. You may draw a diagram to help you answer the question.

Day	Change in Temperature (°F)
2	+6
3	−2
4	+4

3 **Extension** A hiker records the temperature several times during a trip on Mount McKinley. The first measurement is −47.0°F. The table below shows the changes in temperature for the next three measurements.

Measurement	A	B	C
Change in Temperature (°F)	+12.5	−6.0	+8.5

Find the actual temperature at each measurement. Determine the units and intervals for the number line and plot each temperature.

←┼─┼─┼─┼─┼─┼─┼─┼─┼─┼─┼─┼─┼─┼─┼─┼─┼→

1. Which expression is equivalent to $20\left(3p - \frac{3}{5}\right)$?

   (A) $60p - 20\frac{3}{5}$ (C) $60p + 12$

   (B) $60p - 12$ (D) $2\frac{2}{5}p$

2. Which value of the variable is the solution of the equation?

   $24.1 = 13.8 + d$ $d = 11.3, 11.7, 37.9$

   (A) 11.3

   (B) 11.7

   (C) 37.9

   (D) No solution is given in the set of values.

3. Which of the following explains how to get the variable alone on one side of the equation?

   $15z = 8$

   (A) Add 15 to both sides.

   (B) Subtract 15 from both sides.

   (C) Multiply both sides by 15.

   (D) Divide both sides by 15.

4. Which inequality describes the situation? Select all that apply.

   Sara needs a score, s, of more than 90 points on her test to get an A in her math class.

   ☐ $s < 90$

   ☐ $90 < s$

   ☐ $s > 90$

   ☐ $s \geq 90$

   ☐ $90 \leq s$

5. Marco says that $y = 13$ is the solution of the equation $58 - y = 35$. How can you check whether he is correct?

   _____

   _____

   _____

   _____

   _____

6. What is the value of the expression in the table when $m = 7$?

m	$40 - 3m$
3	31
5	25
7	

   _____

7. If $15 + r = 30$, does $15 + r - 15 = 30 - 30$? Explain.

   _____

   _____

   _____

8. Solve the equation.

   $\frac{5}{8}x = 45$

   _____

Name _____

AZ Vocabulary

1. Two numbers that are located on opposite sides of 0 on a number line and are the same distance from 0 are **opposites.**

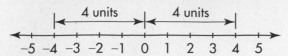

On the number line above, −4 and _____ are on opposite sides of _____.

Each is _____ units from 0, so they are opposites.

2. The counting numbers, their opposites, and zero are **integers.**

15 is an integer because it is a _____ number.

−15 is an integer because it is the opposite of the counting number _____.

−(−15) = _____

3. Write the opposite of each integer.

58 _____

−23 _____

9 _____

4. Circle the integers.

−2.5   0   −9 $\frac{3}{4}$ 16   −4.8

5. On a number line, the positive integers are located to

the _____ of 0.

The negative integers are located to the _____ of 0.

6. Which integer is neither positive nor negative? _____

What is the opposite of this integer? _____

On the Back!

7. Draw a number line from −5 to 5. Label −3 as point *P*. Then write the opposite of −3.

Name _____

1. If two integers are opposites and neither is 0, which statement is NOT true?

    Ⓐ One of the integers is positive and the other is negative.

    Ⓑ The integers are the same distance from 0 on the number line.

    Ⓒ The integers are on opposite sides of 0.

    Ⓓ The integers are equal.

2. Which point on the number line represents the integer -3?

    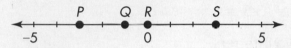

    Ⓐ P

    Ⓑ Q

    Ⓒ R

    Ⓓ S

3. If $x = 7$, what is the value of the expression $3x \cdot (32 - 25)$?

    Ⓐ 21

    Ⓑ 126

    Ⓒ 147

    Ⓓ 647

4. Solve the equation.

    $6n = 42$

    Ⓐ $n = 6$

    Ⓑ $n = 7$

    Ⓒ $n = 8$

    Ⓓ $n = 9$

5. The surface of the Dead Sea is 427 meters below sea level. Use an integer to represent this fact.

    _____

6. What is the opposite of the opposite of -100?

    _____

7. A point is 4 units to the left of 0 on a number line. What is the integer that represents this point?

    _____

8. Evaluate $x^3 + 5(x + 1)$ for $x = 2$.

    _____

9. Solve the equation.

    $n + 18 = 31$

    _____

10. Shing-Yi went to the gym four times last week. If h is the number of hours Shing-Yi spent at the gym each time, write an expression to show how many hours she spent at the gym in all last week.

    _____

D 3·2

A-Z Vocabulary

1. A **rational number** is a number that can be written as a quotient of two integers where the denominator is not equal to 0. $\frac{4}{5}$ and $-\frac{3}{2}$ are rational numbers.

   Is $\frac{999}{1,000}$ a rational number? _____

2. All integers are rational numbers.

   Two ways to write 5 as a quotient of integers are $\frac{5}{1}$ and $\frac{10}{2}$.

   Write 12 as a quotient of integers in two ways.

   _____

3. A decimal like 3.5 is also a rational number. To write this number as

   a quotient, first write it as a mixed number. $3.5 =$ _____

   Now write this number as a quotient of two integers. _____

4. You can plot any rational number on a number line.

   On a horizontal number line, negative numbers are to the

   _____ of 0 and positive numbers are to the _____ of 0.

   On a vertical number line, negative numbers are _____ 0

   and positive numbers are _____ 0.

5. Write the number positioned at point R on the number line below

   as a mixed number. _____

   Write the same number as a decimal. _____

   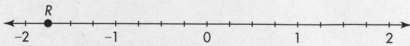

On the Back!

6. Draw a vertical number line. Plot and label point Q (0.6).

Name _____

1. Which number is shown as point *A* on the number line?

A

3.75   3.76

Ⓐ 3.764   Ⓒ 3.758

Ⓑ 3.762   Ⓓ 3.49

2. Which number is located between -3.25 and -3 on a number line?

Ⓐ $-2\frac{3}{4}$ Ⓒ $-3\frac{1}{3}$

Ⓑ $-3\frac{1}{8}$ Ⓓ $-3\frac{1}{2}$

3. Kit read 2 fewer than twice as many books as Tia. Which expression represents the number of books Kit read if *b* represents the books Tia read?

Ⓐ $2(b-2)$

Ⓑ $2b-2$

Ⓒ $2-2b$

Ⓓ $(b \div 2)-2$

4. Which of the following explains how to get the variable alone on one side of the equation?

$18r = 360$

Ⓐ Add 18 to both sides.

Ⓑ Subtract 18 from both sides.

Ⓒ Multiply both sides by 18.

Ⓓ Divide both sides by 18.

5. Label each point on the number line.

0    $\frac{1}{4}$ 1   2

6. Plot -5, $3\frac{1}{2}$, 2, and -4.5 on the number line.

7. Plot each number on the number line.

$\frac{1}{3}$, $1\frac{1}{3}$, $-1\frac{2}{3}$, $-\frac{1}{3}$, $\frac{5}{3}$, $-1\frac{1}{3}$, 0

-3   3

8. Write an inequality that describes this situation. Carolyn's height, *h*, is more than 40 inches.

_____

9. What is the opposite of the opposite of a number? Explain how you know.

_____

_____

_____

_____

_____

Name _____

Vocabulary

1. Remember that the $>$ symbol means **"is greater than"** and the
    $<$ symbol means **"is less than."** The symbols $<$, $>$, and $=$ can
    be used to compare numbers.

    $5 > 2$ $4\frac{1}{2} = 4.5$ $3.25 < 3.5$

    Use $<$, $>$, or $=$ to compare.

    $-1.2 \bigcirc 0$ $\frac{3}{4} \bigcirc \frac{2}{3}$ $\frac{6}{5} \bigcirc 1.2$

2. Use the number line to complete the statement.

    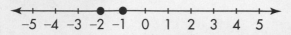

    $-1 \bigcirc -2$ because -1 is to the _____ of -2 on the
    number line.

3. Use $<$, $>$, or $=$ to compare.

    $-5 \bigcirc -4.5$ $\frac{1}{4} \bigcirc -1$ $-2 \bigcirc -\frac{4}{2}$

4. You can also use a number line to order three or more numbers.

    The least number will be farthest to the _____ on the
    number line.

    The greatest number will be farthest to the _____.

5. Plot and label points $P\left(-\frac{5}{2}\right)$, $Q\left(2\frac{3}{4}\right)$, $R\,(1.25)$, and $S\,(-3.5)$ on the
    number line.

    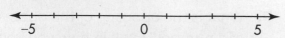

    Use the number line to order the numbers $-\frac{5}{2}$, $2\frac{3}{4}$, 1.25, and -3.5
    from least to greatest.

    _____

On the Back!

6. Use $<$, $>$, or $=$ to compare -8 and -9.

Think Together

Partner Talk

Share your thinking while you work.

Get Started  or

Put ① ② ③ ④ in a bag.
Get paper and a pencil.

For Each Round

Choose A, B, C, D, E, or F.
Pick a tile. Pick two tiles if your group has only two students.
Read the directions next to your tile number.
Discuss: Would it be helpful to think about parts of a dollar?
Decide: Where would each number be on a number line?

A   0.6 $\frac{5}{10}$ 0.4

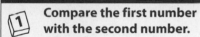

①	Compare the first number with the second number.
②	Compare the second number with the third number.
③	Compare the first number with the third number.
④	Order the numbers from least to greatest.

B $\frac{7}{10}$ $\frac{4}{5}$ 0.6

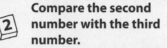

①	Compare the first number with the second number.
②	Compare the second number with the third number.
③	Compare the first number with the third number.
④	Order the numbers from least to greatest.

C $\frac{9}{10}$ $\frac{3}{5}$ 0.7

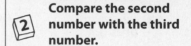

①	Compare the first number with the second number.
②	Compare the second number with the third number.
③	Compare the first number with the third number.
④	Order the numbers from least to greatest.

D $\frac{3}{5}$ 0.8 $\frac{7}{10}$

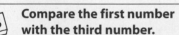

①	Compare the first number with the second number.
②	Compare the second number with the third number.
③	Compare the first number with the third number.
④	Order the numbers from greatest to least.

E $\frac{5}{10}$ $\frac{3}{5}$ 0.3

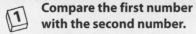

①	Compare the first number with the second number.
②	Compare the second number with the third number.
③	Compare the first number with the third number.
④	Order the numbers from greatest to least.

F $\frac{9}{10}$ $\frac{3}{5}$ 0.8

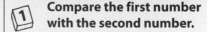

①	Compare the first number with the second number.
②	Compare the second number with the third number.
③	Compare the first number with the third number.
④	Order the numbers from greatest to least.

If you have more time   Make up three numbers you can order by thinking together. Challenge your classmates to think together to order your numbers.

Think Together

Partner Talk
Share your thinking while you work.

Get Started  or

Put ⬚1 ⬚2 ⬚3 ⬚4 in a bag.
Get paper and a pencil.

For Each Round

Choose A, B, C, D, E, or F.
Pick a tile. Pick two tiles if your group has only two students.
Say the two numbers next to your tile number.
Discuss: How do you know if a number is between two other numbers?
Decide: Where is each one of your numbers on a number line?

A Explain why $\frac{1}{2}$ is or is not between the two numbers.

⬚1	0.3 and $\frac{2}{5}$
⬚2	$\frac{3}{10}$ and 0.4
⬚3	0.4 and $\frac{7}{10}$
⬚4	0.4 and 0.6

B Explain why $\frac{7}{10}$ is or is not between the two numbers.

⬚1	$\frac{1}{2}$ and 0.6
⬚2	0.8 and $\frac{9}{10}$
⬚3	0.6 and $\frac{4}{5}$
⬚4	0.5 and $\frac{8}{10}$

C Explain why 0.5 is or is not between the two numbers.

⬚1	0.2 and $\frac{2}{5}$
⬚2	0.6 and $\frac{4}{5}$
⬚3	$\frac{2}{5}$ and 0.7
⬚4	0.4 and $\frac{3}{5}$

D Explain why $\frac{3}{5}$ is or is not between the two numbers.

⬚1	$\frac{2}{5}$ and 0.5
⬚2	0.8 and $\frac{9}{10}$
⬚3	0.5 and $\frac{7}{10}$
⬚4	$\frac{4}{10}$ and 0.8

E Explain why 0.4 is or is not between the two numbers.

⬚1	$\frac{1}{5}$ and $\frac{3}{10}$
⬚2	0.3 and $\frac{1}{2}$
⬚3	$\frac{1}{2}$ and 0.6
⬚4	$\frac{1}{10}$ and 0.5

F Explain why 0.8 is or is not between the two numbers.

⬚1	$\frac{9}{10}$ and 1.0
⬚2	0.5 and $\frac{7}{10}$
⬚3	$\frac{3}{5}$ and 0.7
⬚4	$\frac{3}{5}$ and 0.9

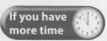 **If you have more time** Make up a "Think Together" question with four other pairs of numbers. Challenge your classmates to think together to answer your question.

Center Game ★★ 3·3

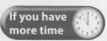

Name _____

1. Which shows the integers in order from least to greatest? Select all that apply.

☐ 1, −2, −6, −11

☐ 1, −11, −6, −2

☐ −11, −2, 1, 6

☐ −11, −6, −2, 1

☐ −2, −6, −11, 1

2. Which of these numbers would be located farthest to the left on a number line?

Ⓐ −0.537

Ⓑ $-\frac{5}{8}$

Ⓒ $-\frac{18}{25}$

Ⓓ −0.725

3. Which inequality is true?

Ⓐ $-\frac{5}{8} > \frac{5}{8}$

Ⓑ $-4.5 > -\frac{9}{2}$

Ⓒ $-\frac{2}{3} > -\frac{3}{4}$

Ⓓ $-3.25 > -3$

4. Which of the following are three solutions of the inequality below?

$x \le 7.001$

Ⓐ 6, 7, 8

Ⓑ 6.999, 7, 7.001

Ⓒ 7, 7.001, 7.002

Ⓓ 7.001, 7.002, 7.003

5. Write an expression to represent 7 less than the quantity 8 times *t*.

_____

6. Order these numbers from greatest to least.

$\frac{9}{10}$, 1.25, $-1\frac{2}{3}$, $\frac{4}{5}$, $-\frac{7}{8}$

_____

7. On two consecutive nights, the low temperature in Chicago was −12°F and −9°F. Write an inequality statement that compares these two temperatures.

_____

8. Solve the equation.

$\frac{3}{5} + y = \frac{2}{3}$

_____

9. Evaluate $8 + x^3 + x$ for $x = 3$.

_____

Name _____

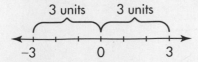 **Vocabulary**

1. The **absolute value** of a number is its distance from 0 on a number line. Distance is always positive.

```
     3 units      3 units
   ┌──────┐    ┌──────┐
 ←─┼──┼──┼──┼──┼──┼──┼──→
   -3        0        3
```

3 is 3 units from 0, so the absolute value of 3 is _____.

−3 is 3 units from 0, so the absolute value of −3 is _____.

The absolute value of 0 is _____.

2. The absolute value of 9 is written as $|9|$, and $|9| =$ _____.

The absolute value of −9 is written as $|-9|$, and $|-9| =$ _____.

How would you read "$|-9|$"? _____

3. Find each absolute value.

$|12| =$ _____

$|-25| =$ _____

$|0| =$ _____

$|4.75| =$ _____

$\left|-\frac{5}{8}\right| =$ _____

4. Find each absolute value and use $<$, $>$, or $=$ to compare.

$|-18| =$ _____ and $|-16| =$ _____, so $|-18|$ ◯ $|-16|$.

$|3.77| =$ _____ and $|-3.76| =$ _____, so $|3.77|$ ◯ $|-3.76|$.

$\left|-4\frac{1}{2}\right| =$ _____ and $\left|-4\frac{5}{8}\right| =$ _____, so $\left|-4\frac{1}{2}\right|$ ◯ $\left|-4\frac{5}{8}\right|$.

On the Back!

5. Find the absolute value of $|-39|$.

Name _____

1. Which is the opposite of 18?

Ⓐ $|-18|$

Ⓑ 0

Ⓒ -18

Ⓓ $|18|$

2. Which statement about absolute value is NOT true?

Ⓐ If two numbers are opposites, they have the same absolute values.

Ⓑ The absolute value of a number is never negative.

Ⓒ The absolute value of a number is always positive.

Ⓓ If two different numbers have the same absolute value, they are the same distance from 0 on the number line.

3. Which number is a possible value for point A on the number line?

Ⓐ 0.25   Ⓒ 1.25

Ⓑ 0.75   Ⓓ 1.75

4. Evaluate this expression for $x = 8$.
$x^2 + 3(x - 4)$

Ⓐ 84   Ⓒ 52

Ⓑ 76   Ⓓ 28

5. Which person's account balance shows a debt greater than $125?

Account	Balance ($)
Trevor	260
Olivia	-65
Charlie	-130
Erin	125

_____

6. Order the numbers from greatest to least.
$|16|, |-14|, |-15|, |13|$

_____

7. Order these fractions from least to greatest.
$\frac{3}{4}, -\frac{2}{3}, \frac{7}{10}, -\frac{5}{6}$

_____

8. Solve $1\frac{3}{4}n = 8\frac{3}{4}$.

_____

9. The thermometer outside Reid's window shows a temperature that is 7 degrees below 0. What is the integer that represents this temperature?

_____

Name _____

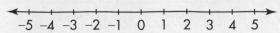 **Vocabulary**

1. A number line can be used to show **integers,** which include the counting numbers (the positive integers), their opposites (the negative integers), and 0.

-5 -4 -3 -2 -1 0 1 2 3 4 5

When comparing two numbers on a horizontal number line, the

greater number will always be to the _____ of the other number.

2. A thermometer is an example of a vertical number line. The negative numbers represent temperatures that are below 0 degrees.

What is the warmest temperature shown on the thermometer

at the right? _____

What is the coldest temperature shown? _____

°F
20
15
10
5
0
-5
-10

3. A thermometer can be used to show changes in temperature. The thermometer at the right shows the temperature getting warmer by 17 degrees.

Which direction on the number line is used to show this change?

_____

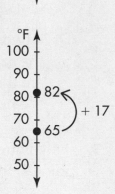

°F
100
90
80 ● 82
70   + 17
● 65
60
50

On the Back!

4. Rachel recorded the temperature at noon in her town every day during a school week. The temperature was 52°F on Monday, 3° warmer on Tuesday, 8° colder on Wednesday, 5° colder on Thursday, and 12° warmer on Friday. How could Rachel use a number line to show these temperature changes and the temperature at noon each day?

Name _____

Algebra: Coordinate Geometry

Topic 4 Standards
6.NS.C.6b, 6.NS.C.6c, 6.NS.C.8, 6.G.A.3
See the front of the Student's Edition for complete standards.

Dear Family,

In this topic, your child will learn about integers and rational numbers and their positions on a coordinate plane. He or she will graph shapes and use absolute value to find distances between the shape's vertices with the same first coordinate or the same second coordinate.

You can help your child understand the concept of a coordinate plane by playing the game below.

Where Am I?

Materials Two sheets of blank paper, pencil

Step 1 Draw a coordinate plane on one sheet of paper with labels. The ordered pairs, such as (−, +), represent the signs of the *x*- and *y*-coordinates in the quadrant.

Step 2 On a second sheet of paper, draw a coordinate plane, but do not include quadrants and ordered pairs. Use this to play the game.

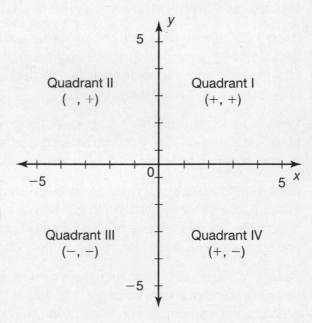

Step 3 Ask your child to identify and locate the quadrant of an ordered pair that you state. Continue until your child correctly identifies the quadrant, and then switch roles.

Step 4 Vary the game by naming a quadrant and asking your child to locate the quadrant and give a possible ordered pair in that quadrant.

Observe Your Child

Focus on Mathematical Practice 6
Attend to precision.

Help your child become proficient with Mathematical Practice 6. Have your child explain the reasoning used to identify the quadrant of each ordered pair using precise mathematical terminology. Clarify misunderstandings or inaccurate use of mathematical language as you play the game.

Álgebra: Geometría de coordenadas

Estándares del Tema 4

6.SN.C.6b, 6.SN.C.6c, 6.SN.C.8, 6.G.A.3

Los estándares completos se encuentran en las páginas preliminares del Libro del estudiante.

Estimada familia:

   En este tema, su niño(a) aprenderá sobre enteros y números racionales, y su posición en un plano de coordenadas. Dibujará figuras y usará el valor absoluto para hallar distancias entre los vértices de las figuras con la misma primera o segunda coordenada.

   Puede ayudar a su niño(a) a entender el concepto de plano de coordenadas al practicar el juego de abajo.

¿Dónde estoy?

Materiales Dos hojas de papel en blanco, lápiz

Paso 1 Dibuje un plano de coordenadas sobre una hoja de papel y rotule. Los pares ordenados, como $(-, +)$ representan los signos de la coordenada *x* y de la coordenada *y* en el cuadrante.

Paso 2 En la segunda hoja de papel, dibuje un plano de coordenadas, pero no incluya cuadrantes ni planos ordenados. Úselo para el juego.

Paso 3 Pida a su niño(a) que identifique y ubique el cuadrante de un par ordenado que usted determine. Continúe hasta que su niño(a) identifique correctamente el cuadrante. Luego, intercambien roles.

Paso 4 Varíe el juego al mencionar un cuadrante y pedirle a su niño(a) que ubique el cuadrante e indique un par ordenado posible en ese cuadrante.

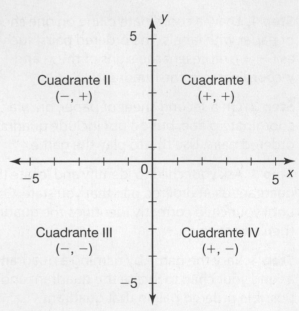

Observe a su niño(a)

Enfoque en la Práctica matemática 6
Prestar atención a la precisión.

Ayude a su niño(a) a adquirir competencia en la Práctica matemática 6. Pida a su niño(a) que explique el razonamiento usado para identificar el cuadrante de cada par ordenado mediante terminología matemática precisa. Clarifique interpretaciones confusas o usos imprecisos del lenguaje matemático mientras juegan.

Name _____

Seismographs

Did You Know? A seismograph is an instrument used to detect and record earthquakes. A seismograph is made of a rotating drum with paper on it, a spring, a weight, and a pen. During an earthquake, the base of the seismograph moves with the motion of the earth. The weight and the pen do not move. As the drum and the paper shake, the pen makes squiggly lines on the paper. The seismograph creates a paper record of an earthquake called a seismogram.

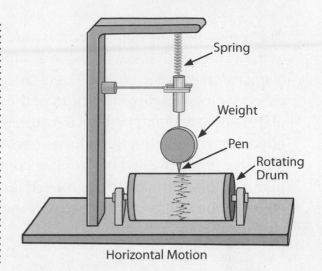

Horizontal Motion

A seismologist reads a seismogram. He or she can tell by looking at the seismogram how far away the earthquake occurred and how strong it was. The epicenter of an earthquake is the point on the Earth's surface directly above where the earthquake actually started in the crust. The seismogram does not show where the epicenter was.

1 To find the epicenter of the earthquake, the seismologist needs to know the locations of two other seismographs that also recorded the earthquake. Plot the location of each seismograph on the coordinate plane.

Seismograph 1 is located at $A(-7\frac{1}{2}, 5\frac{1}{2})$.

Seismograph 2 is located at $B(-7.5, -5.5)$.

Seismograph 3 is located at $C(6.25, 3)$

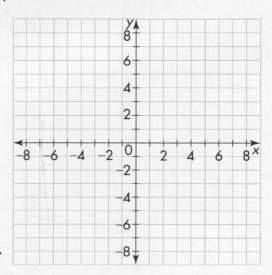

2 The seismologist used the three seismograms and a process called triangulation to determine that the epicenter of the earthquake is at $D(-1.5, -2)$ on the coordinate plane. Graph the location of the epicenter on the coordinate plane.

3 **Extension** Which two points are reflections of each other across one or both of the axes of the coordinate plane?

_____

_____

Name _____

Plate Tectonics

Did You Know? The earth's crust is made up of many pieces that slowly move around and even bump into each other. These pieces are called tectonic plates. The edges of these plates are rough and jagged. Because the edges are rough, they sometimes get stuck together while the rest of the plate continues to move. When the plate has moved far enough, the edges get unstuck and there is an earthquake.

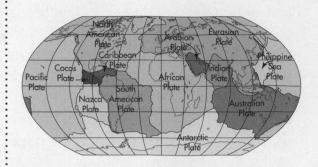

A geologist uses a coordinate plane to map a model of a tectonic plate.

1 A geologist graphs a model of a tectonic plate on a coordinate plane using the points $A(-2, 3.5)$, $B(1.5, 3.5)$, $C(1.5, 1)$, and $D(-2, 1)$. Graph the four points. Then draw polygon $ABCD$.

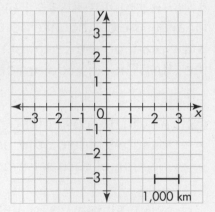

1,000 km

2 What is the perimeter of the tectonic plate $ABCD$?

_____

3 Is polygon $ABCD$ a rectangle? Construct an argument to justify your answer.

_____

_____

_____

_____

_____

_____

Name _____

1. Which of the following explains how to get the variable alone on one side of the equation $\frac{w}{45} = 8$?

   Ⓐ Add 45 to both sides.

   Ⓑ Subtract 45 from both sides.

   Ⓒ Multiply both sides by 45.

   Ⓓ Divide both sides by 45.

2. Which of the following numbers is located between -4.75 and -3.5 on a number line? Select all that apply.

   ☐ $-4\frac{2}{3}$

   ☐ $-3\frac{1}{3}$

   ☐ -4

   ☐ $-4\frac{5}{6}$

   ☐ $-3\frac{3}{4}$

3. Nathan's weight, w, is at most 85 pounds. Which inequality describes Nathan's possible weights?

   Ⓐ $w > 85$

   Ⓑ $w < 85$

   Ⓒ $w \geq 85$

   Ⓓ $w \leq 85$

4. Which inequality is true?

   Ⓐ $-\frac{5}{4} > -\frac{3}{2}$

   Ⓑ $4.83 < 4.82$

   Ⓒ $-5.9 < -6.0$

   Ⓓ $-2\frac{1}{2} > 0$

5. Which person's account balance shows a debt greater than $350?

Account	Balance ($)
Anna	172
Brett	−93
Caleb	−365
Danielle	375

   _____

6. Order the numbers from least to greatest.

   $|24|, |-18|, |-25|, |16|, |0|$

   _____

   _____

7. Solve the equation.

   $\frac{5}{7}y = 20$

   _____

8. Stephanie says that $p = 17$ is the solution of the equation $43 - p = 26$. How can you check whether she is correct? Explain.

   _____

   _____

   _____

   _____

   _____

D 4·1

🄰🅉 Vocabulary

1. A **coordinate plane** is formed by the intersection
   of two number lines called the **x-axis** and **y-axis**.
   Label the axes on the coordinate plane.

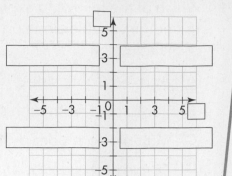

2. The intersection of the axes is at 0 on both number
   lines and is called the **origin**.

   The origin is located at the **ordered pair**

   (_____, _____).

3. The coordinate plane is divided into four **quadrants**.
   Label these on the coordinate plane.

4. To graph any point on the coordinate plane,

   start at the _____.

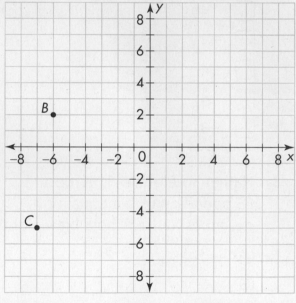

5. To graph the point (3, −2), move _____
   units to the right, then 2 units down.

6. Graph the point (3, −2), and label it A.

7. To write the ordered pair for point B on the

   coordinate plane, start at the _____.

8. The ordered pair that locates point B on the

   coordinate plane is (_____, _____).

9. The reflection of B across the x-axis is the point

   with the ordered pair (_____, _____).

On the Back!

10. Write the ordered pair for point C.

Name _____

1. Which ordered pair locates point *K* on the coordinate plane?

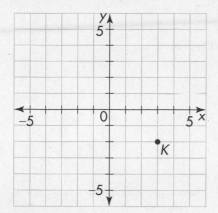

Ⓐ (3, −2)

Ⓑ (−3, 2)

Ⓒ (2, −3)

Ⓓ (−2, 3)

2. In which quadrant is the point (−6, 6) located?

Ⓐ Quadrant I

Ⓑ Quadrant II

Ⓒ Quadrant III

Ⓓ Quadrant IV

3. On a treasure map, there is a point at (5, −2). A note on the map says that to find the treasure, the point must be reflected across the *x*-axis, and then across the *y*-axis. Once that is done, the resulting point will show where the treasure is buried. Which are the coordinates of the point where the treasure is buried?

Ⓐ (5, 0)

Ⓑ (−5, −2)

Ⓒ (2, 0)

Ⓓ (−5, 2)

Use the coordinate plane to answer **4** and **5**.

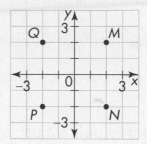

4. What point is located at (−2, 2)?

_____

5. What are the coordinates of point *M*?

_____

6. Graph the inequality $x \geq -2$ on the number line.

$$\longleftarrow\!\!+\!\!+\!\!+\!\!+\!\!+\!\!+\!\!+\!\!+\!\!+\!\!\longrightarrow$$
−4 −3 −2 −1 0 1 2 3 4

7. Solve the equation $24 + n = 61$. Show your work.

_____

_____

_____

8. Order the numbers from least to greatest.

$-0.7, -0.825, -\frac{7}{8}, -\frac{3}{4}$

_____

D 4·2

Name _____

A-Z Vocabulary _____

1. A **rational number** is any number that can be written as a quotient $\frac{a}{b}$, where a and b are integers and b does not equal zero.

   Write each rational number as a quotient of two integers.

   $0.5 = \dfrac{\square}{\square}$ $-3 = -\dfrac{\square}{\square}$ $4\frac{1}{2} = \dfrac{\square}{\square}$

2. An **ordered pair** is a pair of numbers used to locate a point on a coordinate plane. The first number of the pair is the x-coordinate and the second number is the y-coordinate.

   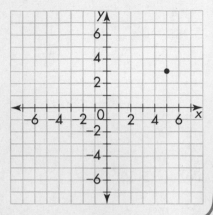

   The ordered pair for the point on the coordinate

   plane on the right is (_____ , _____).

3. The coordinate plane shows the locations of several places in a city. To find the coordinates of the library,

   start at the _____.

   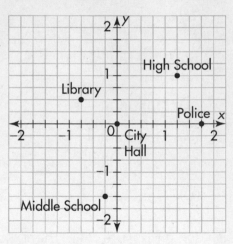

4. The library is 0.75 unit to the left of the origin,

   so the x-coordinate is _____.

5. The library is _____ unit(s) up from the

   x-axis so the y-coordinate is _____.

6. The coordinates of the library are (_____ , _____).

7. Write the x-coordinate of the library as a fraction. _____

8. Write the y-coordinate of the library as a fraction. _____

9. The coordinates of the library, written as fractions, are (_____ , _____).

On the Back!

10. What are the coordinates of the middle school?

Name _____

1. Which ordered pair locates point *M* on the coordinate plane?

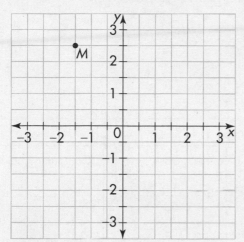

Ⓐ (1.5, 2.5)   Ⓒ (−1.5, 2.5)

Ⓑ (1.5, −2.5)   Ⓓ (−2.5, 1.5)

2. Which ordered pair represents the reflection of point $P\left(-2\frac{3}{4}, 4\frac{1}{2}\right)$ across the *y*-axis?

Ⓐ $\left(2\frac{3}{4}, 4\frac{1}{2}\right)$

Ⓑ $\left(-2\frac{3}{4}, -4\frac{1}{2}\right)$

Ⓒ $\left(2\frac{3}{4}, -4\frac{1}{2}\right)$

Ⓓ $\left(4\frac{1}{2}, -2\frac{3}{4}\right)$

3. Shelley made a map of her neighborhood park. The pool is at (2, 4). The softball field is 2 units directly north of the pool. Which ordered pair describes the location of the softball field?
HINT: Remember to move towards the top of a map to go north.

Ⓐ (0, 4)   Ⓒ (2, 6)

Ⓑ (2, 2)   Ⓓ (4, 4)

4. Graph and label each point on the coordinate plane below.

$R\left(1\frac{1}{4}, -1\frac{3}{4}\right)$

$S(-0.5, -1.5)$

$T(0, -0.75)$

$U(2, 1.5)$

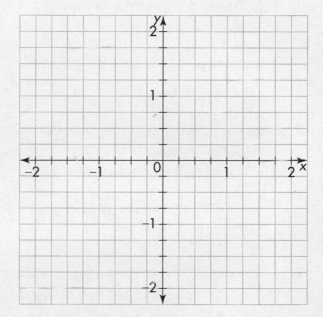

5. Solve the equation.

$3\frac{3}{4}z = 26\frac{1}{4}$

_____

6. What is the opposite of −(−82)?

_____

7. Draw a number line from 0 to 2. Plot the locations of $\frac{3}{8}$, $1\frac{3}{4}$, and 1.25 on the number line.

Name _____

🄰🄯 Vocabulary ————————————————————————

1. The **absolute value** of a number is its distance from zero on a number line. Distance can never be negative, so absolute value is always positive.

   Complete each equation.

   $|-5| =$ _____ $|35| =$ _____

   $|-$ _____ $| = 16$ $|$ _____ $| = 23$

2. The diagram shows the layout of Mrs. Fielding's classroom.

   The room is _____ feet long and

   _____ feet wide.

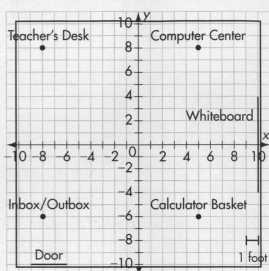

3. How far is Mrs. Fielding's desk from the computer center?
   The coordinates of the desk are (_____, 8).

   The coordinates of the computer center

   are (5, _____).

4. Since the _____ -coordinates are the same, the _____ -coordinates can be used to find the distance between the desk and the computer center.

5. The *x*-coordinate of the desk is _____, so the desk is

   $|-8| =$ _____ feet from the *y*-axis.

6. The *x*-coordinate of the computer center is _____, so the computer center is

   $|5| =$ _____ feet from the *y*-axis.

7. The distance from the desk to the computer center is

   _____ feet + 5 feet = _____ feet.

On the Back!

8. What is the distance from the computer center to the calculator basket?

   $|$ _____ $| + |$ _____ $|$

   = _____ + _____

   = _____ feet

R 4·3

Name _____

1. Between which pair of coordinates is the distance 4 units? Select all that apply.

☐ $(-2, 4)$ and $(2, 4)$

☐ $(4, -2)$ and $(4, -5)$

☐ $(-3, 1)$ and $(-3, 5)$

☐ $(0, -5)$ and $(0, -1)$

☐ $(6, -1)$ and $(2, 1)$

2. Find the distance between the points with coordinates $(5.9, -4.6)$ and $(5.9, 2.7)$.

Ⓐ 1.9 units

Ⓑ 5.9 units

Ⓒ 7.3 units

Ⓓ 8.6 units

3. Which ordered pair represents the reflection of the point $Q(4.7, -5.1)$ across the x-axis?

Ⓐ $(-4.7, 5.1)$

Ⓑ $(4.7, 5.1)$

Ⓒ $(-4.7, -5.1)$

Ⓓ $(5.1, -4.7)$

4. In which quadrant is the point $N\left(-3\frac{2}{3}, -5\frac{1}{4}\right)$ located?

Ⓐ Quadrant I

Ⓑ Quadrant II

Ⓒ Quadrant III

Ⓓ Quadrant IV

5. Find the distance between each pair of points.

$(3, 4)$ and $(3, 9)$ _____

$(6, 2)$ and $(6, 11)$ _____

$(5, 10)$ and $(5, 23)$ _____

6. On a map, a school is located at $(12, -3)$ and a playground is located at $(12, -14)$. If each unit on the map is a city block, how many city blocks is the school from the playground?

_____

7. Graph the inequality on the number line.

$x < 3$

8. Liam says that $q = 8$ is the solution of the equation $2\frac{1}{2}q = 22\frac{1}{2}$. How can you check whether he is correct? Explain.

_____

_____

_____

_____

Name _____

Vocabulary

1. The **perimeter** of a polygon is the distance around its edges. To find perimeter, add all of the side lengths.

   Find the perimeter of the triangle.

   _____ + _____ + _____ = _____

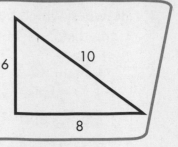

2. The coordinate plane shows the layout of some buildings and a parking lot.

   What distance does each unit of the grid represent?

   _____

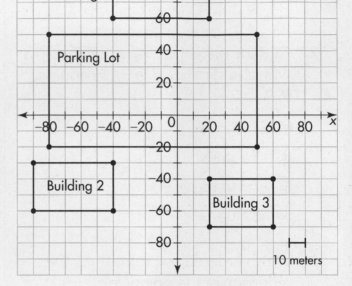

3. The coordinates of the corners of the parking lot, starting from the top left and going clockwise, are:

   (_____, 50), (50, _____),

   (_____, −20), (−80, _____)

4. Find the length of each side of the parking lot, in meters.

   Top: $|-80| +$ |_____| = _____ + 50 = _____ m

   Bottom: |_____| + $|50|$ = 80 + _____ = _____ m

   Left: $|50| +$ |_____| = _____ + 20 = _____ m

   Right: |_____| + $|-20|$ = 50 + _____ = _____ m

5. Add the side lengths to find the perimeter.

   _____ m + 130 m + _____ m + 70 m = _____ m

   The perimeter of the parking lot is _____ meters.

On the Back!

6. What is the perimeter of Building 1?

Teamwork

Partner Talk
Share your thinking while you work.

Get Started  **or**

Get graph paper, a ruler, and a pencil.
Put 1 2 3 4 in a bag.

Repeat for Each Round

Choose **a, b, c, d, e,** or **f**.
Pick a tile. Pick two tiles if your group has only two students.
Do the jobs listed below in order.
To find your job, find the number that matches the tile you chose.

1. **Draw a coordinate plane and label the *x*-axis and *y*-axis from –10 to 10.**

2. **Graph and label the given points.**

3. **Draw line segments to connect the points in the order given. Connect the last point to the first point.**

4. **Find the perimeter of the rectangle that is drawn.**

a. (–3, 2) (1, 2) (1, –2) (–3, –2)	**b.** (0, –5) (0, 5) (4, 5) (4, –5)	**c.** (5, 1) (5, –3) (–1, –3) (–1, 1)
d. (–7, –4) (–7, 2) (2, 2) (2, –4)	**e.** (1, 2) (4, 2) (4, –3) (1, –3)	**f.** (–2, 0) (5, 0) (5, –3) (–2, –3)

 **If you have more time**

Create four new points that can be connected to form a rectangle.
Ask a partner to draw your rectangle on a coordinate plane.

Center Game ★ 4·4

6

Teamwork

Partner Talk

Share your thinking while you work.

 **Get Started**
or

Get graph paper, a ruler, and a pencil.
Put 1 2 3 4 in a bag.

Repeat for Each Round

Choose **a**, **b**, **c**, **d**, **e**, or **f**.
Pick a tile. Pick two tiles if your group has only two students.
Do the jobs listed below in order.
To find your job, find the number that matches the tile you chose.

 1 Draw a coordinate plane and label the *x*-axis and *y*-axis from –10 to 10.

 2 Graph and label the given points.

 3 Determine the quadrant in which each point lies.
Name each point that does not lie in a quadrant and describe its location. Explain.

4 Draw line segments to connect the points in the order given.
Connect the last point to the first. Find the perimeter of the polygon.

a.	(–3, 0) (–3, –5) (1, –5) (1, 0)	**b.**	(3, 0) (3, –3) (–3, –3) (–3, 0)	**c.**	(0, 0) (8, 0) (8, –6) (0, –6)
d.	(2, –3) (2, 4) (6, 4) (6, 0) (8, 0) (8, –3)	**e.**	(–5, 4) (–2, 4) (–2, –3) (1, –3) (1, –6) (–5, –6)	**f.**	(–4, 2) (9, 2) (9, –2) (4, –2) (4, –4) (–4, –4)

If you have more time  Create four new points that can be connected to form a rectangle.
Ask a partner to draw your rectangle on a coordinate plane and find its perimeter.

Center Game ★★ **4·4**

1. What is the perimeter of rectangle *RSTU*?

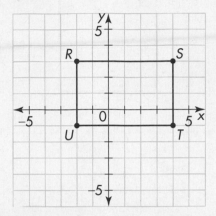

Ⓐ 10 units

Ⓑ 16 units

Ⓒ 20 units

Ⓓ 24 units

2. Square *EFGH* has vertices $E\left(-2\frac{1}{2}, 3\right)$, $F\left(5\frac{1}{2}, 3\right)$, $G\left(5\frac{1}{2}, -5\right)$, and $H\left(-2\frac{1}{2}, -5\right)$. What is the perimeter of *EFGH*?

Ⓐ 8 units

Ⓑ 16 units

Ⓒ 32 units

Ⓓ 64 units

3. Which ordered pair represents the reflection of point $R\left(4\frac{3}{5}, -6\frac{5}{8}\right)$ across both axes?

Ⓐ $\left(-4\frac{3}{5}, -6\frac{5}{8}\right)$

Ⓑ $\left(4\frac{3}{5}, 6\frac{5}{8}\right)$

Ⓒ $\left(6\frac{5}{8}, 4\frac{3}{5}\right)$

Ⓓ $\left(-4\frac{3}{5}, 6\frac{5}{8}\right)$

WXYZ has vertices $W(-7, 2)$, $X(-1, 2)$, $Y(-1, -4)$, and $Z(-7, -4)$.

4. What type of polygon is *WXYZ*?

_____

5. What is the perimeter of *WXYZ*?

_____

6. On a map, Alyssa's house is located at $(8, -9)$ and her school is located at $(8, 3)$. If each unit on the map is a city block, how many city blocks is the school from Alyssa's house?

_____

7. Write an inequality that describes this situation.

At Riverwoods Middle School, the number of students, *s*, in a classroom may not exceed 25.

_____

8. Solve the equation.

$5\frac{2}{3} + p = 9\frac{4}{5}$

_____

9. Evaluate the expression for $n = 9$.

$n^2 + 3(n - 5)$

_____

Name _____

ⒶⓏ Vocabulary

1. A **square** is a rectangle whose side lengths
    are equal. All squares are rectangles, but not all
    rectangles are squares.

    Label the remaining side lengths of the square.

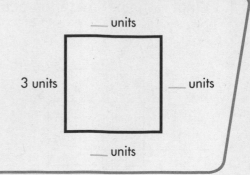

_____ units

3 units

_____ units

_____ units

2. A polygon on a coordinate plane has vertices
    $A(-8, 9)$, $B(7, 9)$, $C(7, -6)$, and $D(-8, -6)$. Graph
    the polygon on the coordinate plane.

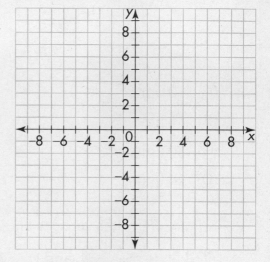

3. Find the side lengths.

    $AB = |\_\_\_\_| + |7| = 8 + \_\_\_\_ = 15$

    $BC = |9| + |\_\_\_\_| = \_\_\_\_ + 6 = \_\_\_\_$

    $CD = |\_\_\_\_| + |-8| = 7 + \_\_\_\_ = \_\_\_\_$

    $DA = |-6| + |\_\_\_\_| = \_\_\_\_ + 9 = \_\_\_\_$

4. All four angles are _____ angles because the sides follow the
    grid lines of the coordinate plane.

5. Is polygon *ABCD* a square? Construct an argument to justify your answer.

    _____

    _____

    _____

On the Back!

6. Triangle *ABC* has vertices $A(-6, -5)$, $B(4, -5)$, and $C(-6, 3)$. Is one
    of the angles of *ABC* a right angle? Explain.

Name _____

Algebra: Patterns and Equations

Topic 5 Standards

6.EE.B.5, 6.EE.C.9

See the front of the Student's Edition for complete standards.

Dear Family,

In this topic, your child will learn how to use variables to represent related quantities in real-world situations. He or she will look for and use patterns to write rules and equations with these variables to describe and extend the patterns. He or she will also represent the patterns using math models, such as tables and graphs on the coordinate plane.

You can help your child understand the concepts of patterns and equations by playing the game below.

What's My Equation?

Materials: Sheets of blank paper, pencil

Help your child relate patterns and equations by playing the game below.

Step 1 Create a table like the one shown. Think of a situation involving money or other quantities that can change by a consistent amount. For example, Chris had $100 in his savings account. Each week, he deposits $40.

Step 2 Complete the table and write an equation that matches the situation. Think of variables to use in writing the equation. In this case, you might write $S = 40w + 100$, where S is the total amount saved after w weeks.

Step 3 Ask your child to identify how much money Chris has saved in all after various numbers of weeks.

Week	Total Amount Saved
Start	$100
1	$140
2	$180
3	
4	
5	
6	

Step 4 Think of a new situation that involves more than one operation. Create a table and write an equation for your new scenario.

Observe Your Child

Focus on Mathematical Practice 6
Attend to precision.

Help your child become proficient with Mathematical Practice 6. Have him or her write out the equation for the table above and solve it using different values for the variable w. Then double check that the answers are correct. Remind him or her of the importance of accuracy when dealing with money.

Álgebra: Patrones y ecuaciones

Estándares del Tema 5

6.EE.B.5, 6.EE.C.9

Los estándares completos se encuentran en las páginas preliminares del Libro del estudiante.

Estimada familia:

   En este tema, su niño(a) aprenderá a usar variables para representar cantidades relacionadas en situaciones de la vida diaria. Buscará y usará patrones para escribir reglas y ecuaciones con esas variables para describir y ampliar los patrones. Luego, usará las reglas y las ecuaciones para extender los patrones. También representará los patrones con modelos matemáticos, como tablas y gráficas en el plano de coordenadas.

   Usted puede ayudar a su niño(a) a comprender el concepto de patrones y ecuaciones con el siguiente juego.

¿Cuál es mi ecuación?

Materiales hojas de papel en blanco, lápiz

Ayude a su niño(a) a relacionar los patrones y las ecuaciones con el siguiente juego.

Paso 1 Creen una tabla como la que se muestra. Piensen en una situación relacionada con el dinero o con cantidades que varíen de manera uniforme. Por ejemplo, Chris tenía $100 en su cuenta de ahorros. Cada semana, deposita $40.

Paso 2 Completen la tabla y escriban una ecuación para representar la situación. Piensen en variables para la ecuación. En este caso, se puede escribir: $A = 40s + 100$, donde A es el total ahorrado después de s semanas.

Paso 3 Pida a su niño(a) que identifique cuánto dinero ahorró Chris después de distintas semanas.

Semana	Total ahorrado
Inicio	$100
1	$140
2	$180
3	
4	
5	
6	

Paso 4 Piensen en una nueva situación que requiera más de una operación. Creen una tabla y escriban una ecuación para la nueva situación.

Observe a su niño(a)

Enfoque en la Práctica matemática 6
Prestar atención a la precisión.

Ayude a su niño(a) a adquirir competencia en la Práctica matemática 6. Pídale que escriba la ecuación de la tabla anterior y que la resuelva con otros valores para la variable *s*. Luego, pídale que compruebe que las respuestas sean correctas. Recuérdele que es importante ser exactos cuando se trata de dinero.

Name _____

Cool Ocean Breezes

Did You Know? Water heats up and cools down relatively slowly because it has a high specific heat value. In contrast, land heats and cools much faster than water. It takes a lot of energy to warm a body of water as large as an ocean. The cool ocean water sucks energy, in the form of heat, from the air over the land. Cool ocean breezes are a result of this temperature difference.

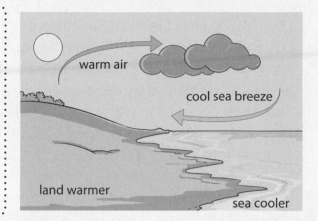

warm air

cool sea breeze

land warmer

sea cooler

Jerred's class is learning about the specific heat value for water. The class observes and records the temperature of a beaker of water as it is heated over time.

Time, t (minutes)	0	5	10	15	20	25
Water Temperature, f (°F)	57	60.7	64.4	68.1	71.8	75.5

▶ Let $t =$ the time in minutes and $f =$ the water temperature in °F. Which is the independent variable? Which is the dependent variable? Explain.

_____

_____

❷ Complete the equation and write a rule that represents the data in the table.

Equation: $f = 0.74t +$ _____

Rule: _____

❸ Use the equation to find the temperature of the water after 30 minutes of heating. Show your work.

_____

❹ **Represent** Emily conducted the same experiment but the temperature of the water at $t = 0$ was 68°F. Every minute that the water was heated, the temperature of the water rose 0.62°F. Write a new equation to represent this situation.

_____

❺ **Extension** Make a table using the equation you wrote in Problem 4.

Name _____

Ocean Currents

Did You Know? Deep ocean currents circle the globe with a force 16 times as strong as all the world's rivers combined. Deep ocean currents are driven by density. When ocean water freezes at the surface of the water, the salt in the water is pushed out into the surrounding water. This water is very cold, salty, and dense. This dense water sinks to the bottom of the ocean. The dense water is replaced by warm water that is less salty and less dense. Deep ocean currents move very slowly but move huge amounts of water.

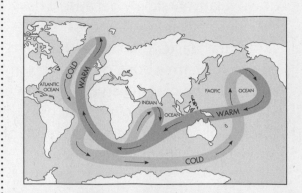

Marla's science class is studying how density and mass are related. They learn mass can be measured in grams (g), and that density can be measured in grams per cubic centimeter (g/cm³).

1 In one classroom experiment, Marla finds that the density of an unknown substance is $\frac{1}{5}$ its mass.

Let d = density and let m = mass.

Complete the table and graph for $d = \frac{m}{5}$.

$d = \frac{m}{5}$	
m (g)	d (g/cm³)
5	
10	
15	

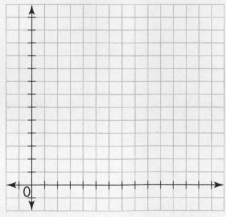

2 **Extension** Marla wants to make 50 cm³ of a saltwater solution that has a density of 1.03 g/cm³. She starts with a mass of 50 grams of water and adds salt to the water in increments of 0.5 gram. How many grams of salt will she need to add to the water to create a solution with the desired density? Use the formula $d = \frac{m}{v}$, where d = density, m = mass of the saltwater solution in grams, and v = 50 cm³. Show your work.

Name _____

1. Which ordered pair locates point Q on the coordinate plane?

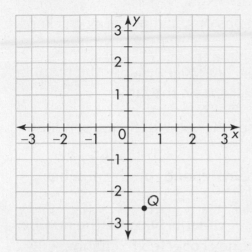

Ⓐ (2.5, −0.5)

Ⓑ (0.5, −2.5)

Ⓒ (−2.5, 0.5)

Ⓓ (−0.5, 2.5)

2. Which ordered pair represents the reflection of point $P\left(-1\frac{4}{5}, -3\frac{2}{3}\right)$ across the x-axis?

Ⓐ $\left(1\frac{4}{5}, -3\frac{2}{3}\right)$

Ⓑ $\left(-3\frac{2}{3}, -1\frac{4}{5}\right)$

Ⓒ $\left(-1\frac{4}{5}, 3\frac{2}{3}\right)$

Ⓓ $\left(1\frac{4}{5}, 3\frac{2}{3}\right)$

3. Which inequality is true?

Ⓐ $-\frac{2}{3} < -\frac{5}{6}$

Ⓑ $8.999 < 8.99$

Ⓒ $-0.3 > 0.2$

Ⓓ $-3\frac{3}{4} > -3\frac{4}{5}$

4. Explain how to get the variable alone on one side of the equation. Then solve the equation.

$r - 37 = 83$

_____

_____

_____

5. Graph the inequality on the number line.

$x > -4$

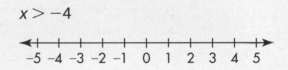

6. Which person's account balance shows a debt greater than $225?

Account	Balance ($)
Maria	235
Robert	−73
Trevor	87
Ella	−230

_____

7. List the absolute values in order from greatest to least.

$|-11|, |17|, |-21|, |0|, |20|$

_____

Name _____

Vocabulary

1. A **dependent variable** is a variable whose value changes in response to another variable.

   The number of eggs, g, produced by a farm depends on the number of chickens, c, on the farm.

   The variable g represents the _____ variable because the number of eggs produced depends on the number of chickens on the farm.

2. An **independent variable** is a variable that causes the value of the dependent variable to change.

   The amount of money, m, collected selling popcorn depends on the number of bags of popcorn, p, sold.

   The variable p represents the _____ variable because the number of bags of popcorn sold causes the amount of money collected to change.

3. A restaurant is offering an omelet special for Sunday brunch. The chef can make a number of omelets, x, for brunch. There are a number of eggs, y, in the restaurant's refrigerator.

   The number of _____ depends on the number of _____.
   Identify each variable: independent variable _____, dependent variable _____

4. Jacob earns \$5 every time his online ad is viewed, v. He earns d dollars from his ad.

   The number of _____ depends on the number of _____.
   Identify each variable: independent variable _____, dependent variable _____

5. Write your own situation where the number of tennis players, p, is an independent variable.

   _____

   _____

   _____

On the Back!

6. Underline the independent variable and circle the dependent variable for the following situation: A book has a number of pages, p. It takes Caroline a number of hours, h, to read the book.

R 5·1

Name _____

1. The manager of a shipping store keeps track of the amount of money, m, collected and the total weight of packages, w, shipped from the store each week. Which best describes the variables m and w?

   Ⓐ The variable m is the independent variable because it affects the total weight of packages, w, shipped each week.

   Ⓑ The variable w is the dependent variable because it depends on the total amount of money, m, collected each week.

   Ⓒ The variable m is the dependent variable because it depends on the total weight of packages, w, shipped each week.

   Ⓓ The variable w is independent of variable m, and the variable m is independent of variable w.

2. In which quadrant is the point $(8.2, -2.8)$ located?

   Ⓐ Quadrant I
   Ⓑ Quadrant II
   Ⓒ Quadrant III
   Ⓓ Quadrant IV

3. Which inequality is represented by the graph below?

   -5 -4 -3 -2 -1 0 1 2 3 4 5

   Ⓐ $x > 4$ Ⓒ $x \geq 4$
   Ⓑ $x < 4$ Ⓓ $x \leq 4$

4. The formula $m = \frac{d}{g}$ can be used to calculate gas mileage, m, in miles per gallon, where g is the number of gallons used to travel a distance of d miles. Use the formula to find the gas mileage of Evan's car if 11 gallons were used to travel 308 miles.

   _____

5. Complete the table.

x	$x + 9$	$2x + 9$	$2(x + 4.5)$
0			
1			
2			
3			

   Which expressions are equivalent?

   _____

   _____

6. Which of these numbers would be located farthest to the left on a number line?

   $\frac{7}{8}, -2\frac{2}{3}, -2.75, \frac{6}{7}, -1\frac{3}{5}$

   _____

7. If $\frac{p}{11} = 22$, does $\left(\frac{p}{11}\right) \times 11 = 22 \times 22$? Explain.

   _____

   _____

   _____

Name _____

A-Z Vocabulary

1. You can use words and numbers to write a **rule** for a number pattern that describes how two variables are related. The rule "multiply *s* by 6 to get *t*" is represented by the equation $6s = t$.

Use the equation $6s = t$ to find the value of *t* when $s = 4$.

$$6s = t$$

$$6(4) = t$$

$$\underline{\hspace{2cm}} = t$$

2. Write a rule to fit the pattern in the table. The rule tells how to use each value for *x* to get the corresponding value for *y*.

x	2	4	6	8
y	3	5	7	9

Think: How can I get to the value of *y* if I start with the value of *x*?

Think: 3 is 1 more than 2.

5 is 1 more than _____.

7 is 1 more than _____.

9 is 1 more than _____.

Write the rule: _____

3. Write an equation to represent the rule.

_____

4. Write a rule and an equation for the pattern in the table.

n	4	5	6	7
m	1	2	3	4

Rule: _____

Equation: _____

On the Back!

5. Write a rule and an equation for the pattern in the table.

p	2	3	5	8
q	10	15	25	40

Toss and Talk

Partner Talk
Share your thinking while you work.

 **Get Started** 👥 or 👥👥

Get 10 squares in one color and 10 in another color.
Get two number cubes. Take turns with another player or team.
Talk about math as you play!

At Your Turn

Toss two number cubes. Add the dots. Find your toss below.
Follow the directions. Explain your thinking. Cover the answer.
If the answer is taken, lose your turn. Have fun!

Toss	Explain how to find an equation that fits the pattern in the table.
2	x: 0 1 2 3 4 y: 4 5 6 7 8
3	x: 0 1 2 3 4 y: 0 3 6 9 12
4	x: 2 3 4 5 6 y: 2 3 4 5 6
5	x: 0 1 2 3 4 y: 0 2 4 6 8
6	x: 0 1 2 3 4 y: 0 4 8 12 16

Toss	
7	x: 1 2 3 4 5 y: 6 7 8 9 10
8	x: 0 1 2 3 4 y: 0 5 10 15 20
9	x: 2 3 4 5 6 y: 0 1 2 3 4
10	x: 0 1 2 3 4 y: 8 9 10 11 12
11	x: 0 3 6 9 12 y: 0 1 2 3 4
12	x: 0 1 2 3 4 y: 6 7 8 9 10

$y = 5 + x$	$y = \frac{x}{3}$	$y = x - 2$	$y = x$
$y = x + 4$	$y = 5x$	$y = 2x$	$y = 4x$
$y = 2x$	$y = 8 + x$	$y = 3x$	$y = 5 + x$
$y = 4x$	$y = x - 2$	$y = 5x$	$y = x + 6$

 How to Win

You win if you are the first to get four connected rectangles, like:

 If you have more time
Play again!

Center Game ★ 5·2

Toss and Talk

Get Started 👥 or 👥👥

Get 10 squares in one color and 10 in another color.
Get two number cubes. Take turns with another player or team.
Talk about math as you play!

At Your Turn

Toss two number cubes. Add the dots. Find your toss below.
Follow the directions. Explain your thinking. Cover the answer.
If the answer is taken, lose your turn. Have fun!

Toss	Explain how to find an equation that fits the pattern in the table.
2	x: 0, 1, 2, 3, 4 / y: 3, 4, 5, 6, 7
3	x: 0, 1, 2, 3, 4 / y: 0, $\frac{1}{2}$, 1, $1\frac{1}{2}$, 2
4	x: 0, 1, 2, 3, 4 / y: 0, 1, 2, 3, 4
5	x: 0, 1, 2, 3, 4 / y: 0, 1.5, 3, 4.5, 6
6	x: 0, 5, 10, 15, 20 / y: 0, 1, 2, 3, 4

Toss	Table
7	x: 0, 1, 2, 3, 4 / y: 0, 2.5, 5, 7.5, 10
8	x: 0, 4, 8, 12, 16 / y: 0, 3, 6, 9, 12
9	x: 0, $\frac{1}{3}$, $\frac{2}{3}$, 1, $1\frac{1}{3}$ / y: $\frac{2}{3}$, 1, $1\frac{1}{3}$, $1\frac{2}{3}$, 2
10	x: 1, 2, 3, 4, 5 / y: $\frac{1}{2}$, $1\frac{1}{2}$, $2\frac{1}{2}$, $3\frac{1}{2}$, $4\frac{1}{2}$
11	x: 3, 6, 9, 12, 15 / y: 1, 2, 3, 4, 5
12	x: 0, 1, 2, 3, 4 / y: 0, 3, 6, 9, 12

$y = \dfrac{x}{5}$	$y = 3 + x$	$y = 1.5x$	$y = x - \dfrac{1}{2}$
$y = \dfrac{1}{3}x$	$y = 2.5x$	$y = x + \dfrac{2}{3}$	$y = \dfrac{3}{4}x$
$y = \dfrac{3}{4}x$	$y = x$	$y = \dfrac{x}{2}$	$y = \dfrac{x}{5}$
$y = x + \dfrac{2}{3}$	$y = 1.5x$	$y = 2.5x$	$y = 3x$

How to Win You win if you are the first to get four connected rectangles, like:

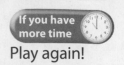

If you have more time

Play again!

Center Game ★★ 5·2

Name _____

1. Which equation best represents the data in the table?

m	3	5	8	12
n	11	13	16	20

Ⓐ $n = 2m$

Ⓑ $n = m + 8$

Ⓒ $m = n + 8$

Ⓓ $n = \frac{5}{3}m$

2. Which value of the variable is the solution to $45.2 = 18.9 + p$?

$p = 23.5, 26.3, 64.1$

Ⓐ 23.5

Ⓑ 26.3

Ⓒ 64.1

Ⓓ No solution is given in the set of values.

3. Which expression is equivalent to $24\left(3d - \frac{5}{8}\right)$?

Ⓐ $72d + 15$

Ⓑ $72d - 15$

Ⓒ $72d - 24\frac{5}{8}$

Ⓓ $2\frac{3}{8}d$

4. Evaluate this expression for $z = 7$.

$2z^2 + 5(z - 3)$

Ⓐ 69

Ⓑ 78

Ⓒ 118

Ⓓ 216

5. Square PQRS has vertices $P(-1, 4)$, $Q(6, 4)$, $R(6, -3)$, and $S(-1, -3)$. What is the perimeter of square PQRS?

_____

Use the text and table to answer **6** and **7**.

Laura and Josh bought sweet corn at a local farm. The table shows the number of ears of corn purchased, *e*, and the total price, *p*.

Number of Ears, e	Total Price, p
5	$1.95
8	$3.12
12	$4.68
15	$5.85

6. Identify the independent variable and the dependent variable.

Independent variable: _____

Dependent variable: _____

7. Write an equation that represents the pattern in the table.

_____

8. Write an inequality that describes this situation.

To be eligible to vote in a national election, a U.S. citizen must be at least 18 years old. Let *a* represent the age of an eligible U.S. voter.

_____

Name _____

Vocabulary

1. A **variable** is a letter or symbol that represents an unknown quantity. In the equation $y = 7x - 3$, the variables are _____ and _____.

2. You can use **substitution** to replace a variable in an algebraic expression with a number. Use substitution to find the value of the expression $4x + 1$ when $x = 5$.

   $4x + 1$

   $= 4(\underline{\qquad}) + 1$

   $= \underline{\qquad}$

3. Katelyn earns 2 points for each question answered correctly on a math quiz, plus 5 extra credit points.

   Write an expression that describes how to find Katelyn's score. Let q represent the number of questions answered correctly.

   2 points for each question answered correctly, plus 5 extra credit points

   ↓   ↓   ↓   ↓   ↓

   _____ × _____   + _____

4. Complete the table to show how Katelyn's quiz score is related to the number of questions she answers correctly. Substitute values of q into the expression to find values of the score, s.

Questions Answered Correctly, q	$2q + 5$	Score, s
0	$2(0) + 5$	5
1	$2(\underline{\quad}) + 5$	_____
2	$2(\underline{\quad}) + 5$	_____

5. Write and solve an equation that can be used to find Katelyn's score, s, if she answers 9 questions correctly. _____

On the Back!

6. Use the equation $d = 4c + 8$ to complete the table.

c	0	1	2	3
d				

R 5·3

Name _____

1. Which equation can be used to describe the pattern in the table? Select all that apply.

r	3	4	5	6	7
s	9	8	7	6	5

☐ $s = 12 - r$

☐ $s - r = 6$

☐ $r - s = 2$

☐ $r = 12 - s$

☐ $r + s = 12$

2. Which of these numbers is located farthest to the left on a number line?

Ⓐ -0.625　　Ⓒ $-\frac{11}{15}$

Ⓑ $-\frac{7}{8}$　　Ⓓ -0.75

3. Which expression is **NOT** equivalent to the given expression?

$42y - 8 - 18y$

Ⓐ $4(6y - 2)$　　Ⓒ $6(4y - 2)$

Ⓑ $2(12y - 4)$　　Ⓓ $8(3y - 1)$

4. On a map, Ryan's house is located at $(-8, 5)$ and his friend Zach's house is located at $(-8, -7)$. If each unit on the map represents a city block, how many blocks is Zach's house from Ryan's?

Ⓐ 2 city blocks

Ⓑ 3 city blocks

Ⓒ 12 city blocks

Ⓓ 16 city blocks

5. Use the equation to complete the table.

$y = 4x - 3$

x	y
1	
3	
5	
8	
10	

6. Solve the equation.

$\frac{5}{7}z = 45$

7. Between which two points is the distance 8 units?

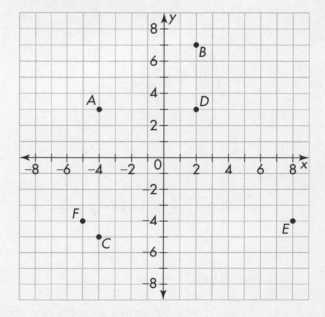

Vocabulary

1. The graph of a **linear equation** is a straight line. Notice that the word *line* is in the word *linear*.

   The graph of $y = x + 4$ is a straight line, so $y = x + 4$ is a _____ equation.

2. Complete the table using the equation $b = a - 1$. First, choose two more values for a. Then use the equation to find each corresponding value of b.

   $b = a - 1$

   $b = 1 - 1 = 0$

   $b = \underline{\quad} - 1 = \underline{\quad}$

   $b = \underline{\quad} - 1 = \underline{\quad}$

$b = a - 1$	
a	b
1	0
_____	_____
_____	_____

3. Write each pair of values in the table as an ordered pair (a, b).

   _____

4. Graph each ordered pair on the coordinate plane. Then draw a line through the points. The point $(1, 0)$ has been graphed for you.

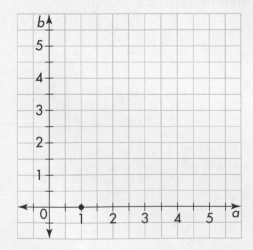

On the Back!

5. Ernie drew a rectangle with an area, a, that was 2 times its width, w. Use the equation $a = 2w$ and the values $w = 1$, $w = 2$, and a third value of your choice to make a table. Then use the table to make a graph.

Name _____

1. Which equation represents the graph below?

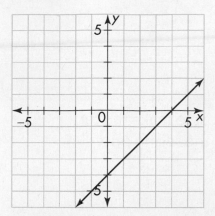

Ⓐ $y = 4x$ Ⓒ $y = 4 - x$

Ⓑ $y = x + 4$ Ⓓ $y = x - 4$

2. Rectangle *WXYZ* has vertices $W(-5, 3)$, $X(3, 3)$, $Y(3, -2)$, and $Z(-5, -2)$. What is the perimeter of rectangle *WXYZ*?

Ⓐ 20 units   Ⓒ 32 units

Ⓑ 26 units   Ⓓ 40 units

3. Which rule fits the pattern in the table?

m	0	$\frac{1}{2}$	1	$1\frac{1}{2}$	2
n	0	$1\frac{1}{2}$	3	$4\frac{1}{2}$	6

Ⓐ The value of *n* is 3 less than the value of *m*.

Ⓑ The value of *n* is 3 more than the value of *m*.

Ⓒ The value of *n* is 3 times the value of *m*.

Ⓓ The value of *n* is $\frac{1}{3}$ the value of *m*.

4. What is the opposite of $|-27|$?

_____

5. Solve the equation $\frac{q}{11} = 19$.

_____

6. Hannah is renting a truck for her move to a new apartment. The rental company charges $40 for the truck, plus $35 for each hour the truck is used. Write an equation that describes the relationship between the cost, *c*, in dollars, of the truck rental, and the number of hours, *h*, for which it is rented.

_____

7. Use the equation from Problem 6 to complete the table by finding the cost of renting a truck for 5 hours.

Hours, *h*	2	3	4	5
Cost ($), *c*	110	145	180	

8. What ordered pair represents the reflection of the point $\left(4\frac{3}{8}, -6\frac{1}{4}\right)$ across both axes?

_____

Name _____

A-Z Vocabulary

1. Use the **order of operations** to evaluate an expression with more than one operation. First, multiply and divide in order from left to right. Then, add and subtract in order from left to right.

   Evaluate $3x - 2$ for $x = 5$.

   $3x - 2 = 3(5) - $ _____ $= $ _____ $= $ _____

2. A store sells a toy car for $1 less than twice what it cost to make the car. Write an equation to represent the situation. Let $s = $ the selling price and $c = $ the cost to make the car.

   selling price = 2 times the cost minus $1

   $s = $ _____ $\times$ _____ $- $ _____

3. Use the equation you wrote in Exercise 2 to complete the table of values and draw a graph.

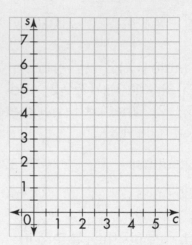

$s = $ _____	
c	s
2	_____
3	_____
4	7

4. What is the selling price of a toy car that cost $4 to make? _____

On the Back!

Write an equation, make a table, and then graph to solve.

5. Walter pays $4 for each gallon, g, of gas for his lawnmower. He uses a gift card worth $5 to reduce the amount of his purchase. How much money, m, will he spend in all if he buys 4 gallons of gas? Write an equation, make a table using the values of 2, 3, and 4 for g, and then graph to solve the problem.

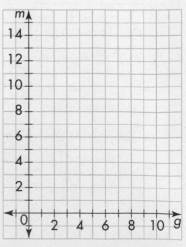

R 5·5

Display the Digits

Partner Talk
Share your thinking while you work.

Get Started
👤 or 👥

Pick a tile. Find the linear equation next to that number.
Find the graph of that equation. Explain your choice.
Place your tile on the graph. Display each 0–9 tile exactly once.
If you have a partner, take turns.

0	$y = x + 2$
1	$y = 2x + 2$
2	$y = \frac{x}{3} + 2$
3	$y = \frac{x}{2} + 1$
4	$y = 2x - 1$
5	$y = \frac{x}{2} - 1$
6	$y = 3x - 2$
7	$y = \frac{x}{3} - 2$
8	$y = 3x + 2$
9	$y = 2x + 1$

a.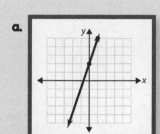

b.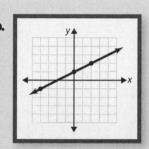

c.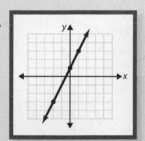

d.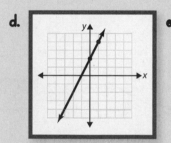

e.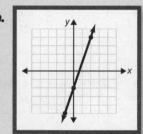

f.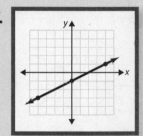

g.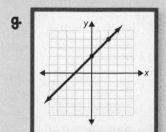

h.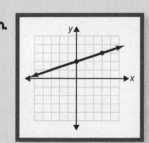

i.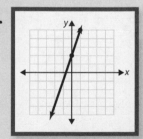

j.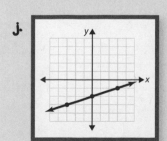

k.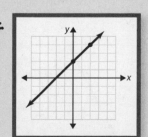

l.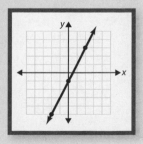

If you have more time
Make up three equations of straight lines and draw their graphs.
Ask your partner to match each equation with its graph.

Center Game ★ 5-5

Display the Digits

Partner Talk
Share your thinking while you work.

 **Get Started**
👤 or 👥

Pick a tile. Find the graph next to that number.
Find the equation of that line. Explain your choice.
Place your tile on the equation. Display each 0–9 tile exactly once.
If you have a partner, take turns.

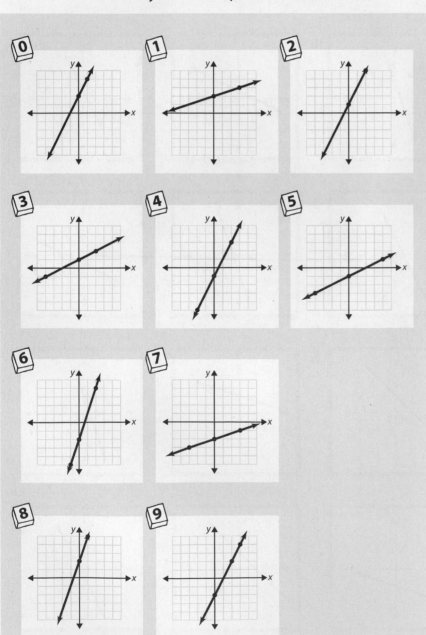

$y = 3x + 2$

$y = \frac{x}{2} + 1$

$y = \frac{x}{3} + 2$

$y = 3x - 2$

$y = \frac{x}{2} - 1$

$y = 2x + 2$

$y = 2x + 1$

$y = 2x - 2$

$y = \frac{x}{3} - 2$

$y = 2x - 1$

 **If you have more time**

Make up three graphs of straight lines and write their equations.
Ask your partner to match each graph with its equation.

Center Game ★★ 5•5

Name _____

1. Which equation best represents the data in the table?

x	y
0	2
3	3
6	4

Ⓐ $y = 2 + x$

Ⓑ $y = \frac{x}{3}$

Ⓒ $y = 2 + \frac{x}{3}$

Ⓓ $y = 2 + 3x$

2. Which ordered pair represents a point on the line of the equation $y = \frac{1}{4}x + 3$? Select all that apply.

☐ $(1, 4)$

☐ $(0, 3)$

☐ $\left(3, 2\frac{3}{4}\right)$

☐ $\left(2, 3\frac{1}{2}\right)$

3. A store places out-of-season clothes on sale. The sales price is $\frac{1}{3}$ of the original price, x. Which expression describes the new sales price?

Ⓐ $x - \frac{1}{3}$

Ⓑ $x + \frac{1}{3}$

Ⓒ $x \div \frac{1}{3}$

Ⓓ $\frac{1}{3}x$

4. How many terms does the expression $9^2 - 4 \times 5 + 12 \div 2$ have?

Ⓐ 2 terms   Ⓒ 4 terms

Ⓑ 3 terms   Ⓓ 5 terms

5. What number is located between -3.95 and -3.94 on a number line?

_____

6. Complete the table for the equation $y = 2x - 1$.

x	y
1	
2	
3	

7. Use the table data from Exercise 6 to graph the equation $y = 2x - 1$.

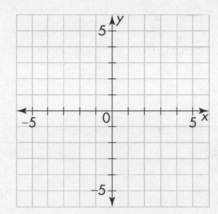

8. What is the value of the expression $3x - 4y + 2z^2$ when $x = 7$, $y = 3$, and $z = 5$?

_____

9. What part of the expression $\frac{m}{3} - 4n + 7$ is a quotient? Describe its parts.

_____

_____

_____

Name _____

A-Z Vocabulary

1. A **math model,** such as a table, graph, or equation, can be used to represent a problem situation mathematically.

   The perimeter, p, of a square is 4 times the length of one of its sides, s.

   Write an equation to model the perimeter of a square. _____

2. Dion needs 602 square feet of wallpaper. Each roll of wallpaper covers 56 square feet. How many rolls of wallpaper does Dion need?

   Model the problem with a table.

3. What equation can you write to represent the total square feet of wallpaper, s, for r rolls of wallpaper?

   _____

Number of Rolls	Total Square Feet
1	56
2	2 × _____ = _____
4	_____ × _____ = _____
8	_____ × _____ = _____
10	_____ × _____ = _____

4. Use the equation you wrote to solve for r when s = 602. Show your work.

   _____

5. If the store only sells whole rolls of wallpaper, how many rolls should Dion buy? Explain.

   _____

   _____

   _____

On the Back!

6. Cory is filling a large aquarium tank with a hose. The level of the water in the tank rises 4.5 inches each hour. The tank already has 8 inches of water in it. How many hours will it take to fill the tank to a depth of 35 inches? Make a table and write an equation to model and solve the problem.

Fluently Divide Whole Numbers

Topic 6 Standards

6.NS.B.2, 6.EE.A.2c, 6.EE.B.7

See the front of the Student's Edition for complete standards.

Dear Family,

Your child is learning to use the standard algorithm for division to divide multi-digit numbers. He or she will use estimation to determine where to place the first digit in the quotient and to check whether the quotient is reasonable. Your child will continue to practice this skill by evaluating expressions and solving equations that involve division.

Here is an activity you can do with your child to help him or her develop fluency with multi-digit division.

Estimating Quotients

Materials: Number cube

Step 1 Roll a number cube six times. Write one four-digit number and one two-digit number using the digits you rolled.

Step 2 Write a division expression using the two numbers, such as 2,361 ÷ 12. Estimate the quotient and then divide.

Step 3 Choose an estimate, such as 100 or 50. Challenge your child to write a division expression with two- and four-digit numbers that will result in a quotient as close to the estimate as possible.

Observe Your Child

Focus on Mathematical Practice 2
Reason abstractly and quantitatively.

Help your child become proficient with Mathematical Practice 2. Ask him or her to tell you the division fact that he or she used to determine compatible numbers for the estimate in the activity above.

Nombre _____

Dividir números enteros con facilidad

Estándares del Tema 6

6.SN.B.2, 6.EE.A.2c, 6.EE.B.7

Los estándares completos se encuentran en las páginas preliminares del Libro del estudiante.

Estimada familia:

Su niño(a) está aprendiendo a usar el algoritmo convencional de la división para dividir números de varios dígitos. Usará la estimación para determinar dónde ubicar el primer dígito del cociente y comprobar si el cociente es razonable. Su niño(a) seguirá practicando esta destreza al evaluar expresiones y resolver ecuaciones de división.

Esta es una actividad que puede realizar con su niño(a) para desarrollar fluidez en la división de números de varios dígitos.

Estimar cocientes

Materiales cubo numérico

Paso 1 Lancen un cubo numérico seis veces. Escriban un número de cuatro dígitos y un número de dos dígitos usando los dígitos que salieron en el lanzamiento.

Paso 2 Escriban una expresión de división usando los dos números, como $2,361 \div 12$. Estimen el cociente y, luego, dividan.

Paso 3 Escojan una estimación, como 100 o 50. Anime a su niño(a) a escribir una expresión de división con números de dos y cuatro dígitos que tenga como resultado un cociente que esté lo más cerca posible de la estimación.

Observe a su niño(a)

Enfoque en la Práctica matemática 2
Razonar de manera abstracta y cuantitativa.

Ayude a su niño(a) a adquirir competencia en la Práctica matemática 2. Pídale que le explique la operación de división que usó para hallar números compatibles para la estimación de la actividad anterior.

Name _____

Divide Multi-Digit Numbers

1. $24\overline{)168}$ **2.** $37\overline{)333}$ **3.** $82\overline{)164}$ **4.** $97\overline{)582}$

5. $58\overline{)470}$ **6.** $71\overline{)156}$ **7.** $95\overline{)4,180}$ **8.** $49\overline{)1,372}$

9. $62\overline{)4,216}$ **10.** $15\overline{)1,065}$ **11.** $98\overline{)9,038}$ **12.** $14\overline{)11,816}$

13. $88\overline{)21,208}$ **14.** $53\overline{)27,613}$ **15.** $19\overline{)18,715}$ **16.** $72\overline{)38,990}$

17. A school auditorium has 560 seats. Each row in the auditorium has 35 seats. How many rows are in the auditorium? Show how you know.

Name _____

Divide Multi-Digit Numbers

1. 55)495

2. 63)189

3. 22)154

4. 62)124

5. 75)201

6. 11)856

7. 76)5,548

8. 42)2,562

9. 44)1,276

10. 42)1,554

11. 91)1,095

12. 96)11,136

13. 93)18,135

14. 82)13,366

15. 89)32,129

16. 38)25,154

17. Write one digit in each box to complete the division problem. You will not use the same digit twice.

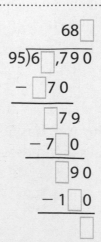

Name _____

Divide Multi-Digit Numbers

1. 77)231   **2.** 91)637   **3.** 43)215   **4.** 73)146

5. 87)323   **6.** 11)239   **7.** 68)1,224   **8.** 18)1,422

9. 73)2,263   **10.** 48)1,200   **11.** 11)1,041   **12.** 92)20,056

13. 86)11,008   **14.** 72)60,336   **15.** 29)11,426   **16.** 69)45,764

17. One whole number is divided by a second whole number, resulting in a quotient that is also a whole number. The dividend has three digits, and the quotient has one digit. How many digits does the divisor have? Explain.

Name _____

Divide Multi-Digit Numbers

1. $76\overline{)380}$ **2.** $33\overline{)231}$ **3.** $89\overline{)356}$ **4.** $68\overline{)544}$

5. $43\overline{)364}$ **6.** $31\overline{)201}$ **7.** $37\overline{)3,626}$ **8.** $75\overline{)6,525}$

9. $24\overline{)1,800}$ **10.** $32\overline{)1,088}$ **11.** $63\overline{)2,208}$ **12.** $33\overline{)25,047}$

13. $66\overline{)38,478}$ **14.** $42\overline{)10,164}$ **15.** $27\overline{)14,715}$ **16.** $51\overline{)22,859}$

17. A rectangular field has an area of 7,154 square feet. The field is 73 feet long. What is the width of the field? Show how you know.

Divide Multi-Digit Numbers

1. 79)474

2. 75)300

3. 82)164

4. 58)406

5. 49)382

6. 22)232

7. 86)8,428

8. 31)2,635

9. 95)5,890

10. 32)1,184

11. 55)3,369

12. 45)16,425

13. 98)83,594

14. 36)27,684

15. 98)40,278

16. 72)16,796

---

17. A four-digit whole number is divided by a two-digit whole number. The digit in the ones place of the dividend is 8. The digit in the ones place of the divisor is 6. The quotient is a whole number with no remainder. What digit(s) could be in the ones place of the quotient? Explain.

Name _____

Divide Multi-Digit Numbers

1. 23)207

2. 59)177

3. 56)280

4. 91)364

5. 73)629

6. 25)876

7. 99)6,039

8. 92)8,188

9. 41)1,353

10. 42)2,772

11. 31)2,634

12. 36)33,228

13. 48)20,688

14. 55)28,380

15. 26)19,942

16. 89)29,070

17. For a fundraiser, the students of a middle school raised a total of $22,126. If each student raised $37, how many students are in the middle school? Show how you know.

Name _____

Conserving Water

Did You Know? About 70% of water used in households is used indoors. The bathroom is where most of the indoor water is used. There are many ways to conserve water in the bathroom. Shutting off the faucet while brushing teeth can save more than 50 gallons of water each week.

Indoor Water Use

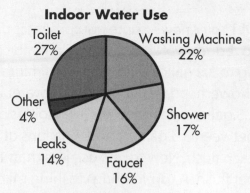

1. A leaking toilet wastes up to 200 gallons of water each day. Jonas writes the equation $r = \frac{g}{t}$ to calculate the leak rate, r, in gallons per hour. The number of gallons that leak out is g and the total time of the leak is t.

   What is the leak rate, in gallons per hour, of the toilet?

   _____

2. **Represent** Caroline conserves 1,300 gallons of water by shutting off the faucet while brushing her teeth. For about how many weeks has Caroline been shutting off the faucet while brushing her teeth?

   _____

3. **Extension** A hotel has 15 leaking faucets, 12 leaking toilets, and 1 leaking sprinkler. Each faucet wastes 42 gallons per week. Each toilet wastes 63 gallons per week. The sprinkler wastes 84 gallons each week. As part of her weekly report, the hotel manager writes an expression to calculate the number of gallons of water wasted each day, g.

   Write and evaluate an expression to find how much water would be saved each day by fixing the leaks.

   _____

   _____

Name _____

Reducing Water Usage

Did You Know? Some equipment is designed to reduce water use. A showerhead can spray up to 2.2 gallons of water each minute. A showerhead designed to save water uses only 1.5 gallons per minute. Older toilets might use between 3.5 gallons and 7 gallons of water for each flush. New toilets use less than 1.3 gallons per flush. A top-loading washing machine might use 40 gallons of water to wash a load of clothes. A front-loading washing machine can use half of that.

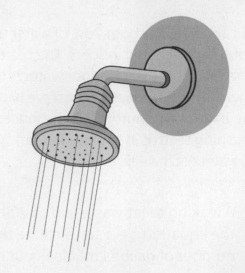

1 Keiko's younger sister shortens her showers from 10 minutes long to 7 minutes long in order to conserve water. If her showerhead sprays 2 gallons of water per minute, how much water does Keiko's sister conserve per shower?

_____

2 Last week, Keiko used 560 gallons of water for baths. Each bath used 70 gallons of water. How many baths did Keiko take last week?

_____

3 **Represent** This week, Keiko switches from taking baths to taking showers. If Keiko takes 9-minute showers, how many showers could she take this week and still use less water than the water used taking baths last week? Write an expression to represent the situation. Then evaluate to answer the question.

_____

_____

4 **Extension** Keiko's family has a washing machine that uses 20 gallons of water per load. How many loads of laundry can Keiko's family wash with the water saved in one week by Keiko switching from baths to showers? Assume Keiko plans to take the same number of showers as she took baths.

_____

Name _____

1. Find the distance between two points with coordinates $(-2.6, -4.7)$ and $(-2.6, 4.7)$.

Ⓐ 2.6 units   Ⓒ 7.3 units

Ⓑ 5.2 units   Ⓓ 9.4 units

2. Which ordered pair represents the reflection of point $Q\left(-5\frac{7}{8}, -3\frac{2}{5}\right)$ across the x-axis?

Ⓐ $\left(5\frac{7}{8}, -3\frac{2}{5}\right)$

Ⓑ $\left(5\frac{7}{8}, 3\frac{2}{5}\right)$

Ⓒ $\left(-5\frac{7}{8}, 3\frac{2}{5}\right)$

Ⓓ $\left(-3\frac{2}{5}, 5\frac{7}{8}\right)$

3. Which expression is equivalent to $27\left(3t - \frac{4}{9}\right)$?

Ⓐ $72d + 15$

Ⓑ $81t - 12$

Ⓒ $81t - 27\frac{4}{9}$

Ⓓ $2\frac{5}{9}t$

4. Which rational number is located between -7.83 and -7.82 on a number line?

Ⓐ -7.81 Ⓒ -7.831

Ⓑ -7.828 Ⓓ -7.84

5. What is the value of the expression $2a - 5b + 3c^2$ when $a = 7$, $b = 2$, and $c = 4$?

Ⓐ 17   Ⓒ 56

Ⓑ 52   Ⓓ 148

6. Complete the table for the equation $y = 3x + 4$.

x	y
0	
1	
2	
3	

7. Use the data in the table from Exercise 6 to graph the equation $y = 3x + 4$.

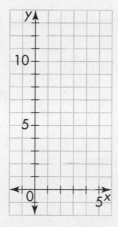

8. Eric says that $q = 29$ is the solution of the equation $67 - q = 48$. How can you check whether he is correct?

_____

_____

_____

_____

_____

_____

Name _____

A-Z Vocabulary

1. **Compatible numbers** are numbers that are easy to compute mentally and can be used to estimate solutions to problems.

   Estimate 2,529 ÷ 24.

   First, find compatible numbers.

   2,529 is close to _____ , and 24 is close to _____ .

   Divide using the compatible numbers you chose.

   _____ ÷ _____ = _____ .   So, 2,529 ÷ 24 is about _____ .

2. How many buses are needed for 1,584 students if each bus can hold 72 students?

   Write an expression to represent the problem.   _____ ÷ _____

3. Find compatible numbers for the numbers in the expression.

   1,584 is close to _____ .   72 is close to _____ .

4. Rewrite the expression using the compatible numbers. Then divide to solve the problem.

   _____ ÷ _____   About _____ buses are needed.

5. There can be more than one reasonable estimate when using compatible numbers. Use two pairs of compatible numbers to find two different estimates for 9,741 ÷ 276.

   9,741 is close to _____ .   9,741 is close to _____ .

   276 is close to _____ .   276 is close to _____ .

6. Rewrite each expression using the compatible numbers. Then divide.

   _____ ÷ _____ = _____   _____ ÷ _____ = _____

7. So, 9,741 ÷ 276 is about _____ or _____ .

On the Back!

8. Estimate using compatible numbers.

   4,673 ÷ 74

R 6·1

Name _____

1. Which points are located in Quadrant III of a coordinate plane? Select all that apply.

   ☐ $(-5.75, -2)$

   ☐ $(-7, 2.5)$

   ☐ $\left(3\frac{1}{3}, -2\frac{2}{3}\right)$

   ☐ $\left(-3\frac{1}{3}, -2\frac{2}{3}\right)$

   ☐ $(5.75, 2.5)$

2. A warehouse gets a delivery of 3,456 boxes. The boxes are then equally distributed to 72 stores. Which is the best estimate of the number of boxes each store receives?

   Ⓐ 35

   Ⓑ 40

   Ⓒ 50

   Ⓓ 70

3. Which of these numbers is located farthest to the right on a number line?

   Ⓐ -0.272

   Ⓑ $-\frac{5}{16}$

   Ⓒ -0.375

   Ⓓ $-\frac{7}{25}$

4. Which inequality describes the situation?

   Victoria's test score, t, must be at least 65.

   Ⓐ $t > 65$

   Ⓑ $t < 65$

   Ⓒ $t \geq 65$

   Ⓓ $t \leq 65$

5. Graph and label each point on the coordinate plane below.

   $P\left(-1\frac{1}{4}, \frac{1}{2}\right)$

   $Q(0.75, -1.25)$

   $R\left(1\frac{3}{4}, 0\right)$

   $S(-2, -0.75)$

   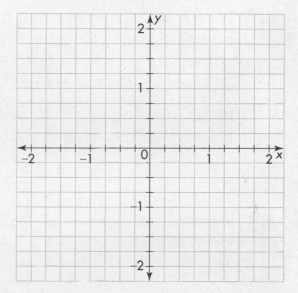

6. Solve the equation $\frac{5}{8}p = 25$.

   _____

7. Order the numbers from greatest to least.

   $|24|, |-25|, |-21|, |19|$

   _____

8. What is the opposite of -129?

   _____

D 6·2

Name _____

Vocabulary

1. A **remainder** is the whole number that is left after dividing. The remainder is always less than the divisor. In the division problem at the right, the remainder is 1.

$$\begin{array}{r} 5\ R1 \\ 3\overline{)16} \\ -15 \\ \hline 1 \end{array}$$

   Write the remainder for each division problem.

   $$\begin{array}{r} 2\ R\text{\_\_\_\_\_} \\ 6\overline{)14} \end{array} \qquad \begin{array}{r} 8\ R\text{\_\_\_\_\_} \\ 5\overline{)44} \end{array} \qquad \begin{array}{r} 11\ R\text{\_\_\_\_\_} \\ 7\overline{)83} \end{array}$$

2. A charity takes donations to purchase livestock for struggling farms. The table shows the prices of some of the animals available. A sixth-grade class raised $2,758 for the charity.

Animal	Price
Flock of Chicks	$22
Flock of Ducks	$24
Honeybees	$31
Rabbit	$63

   Write a division expression to represent the number of rabbits that can be purchased.

   _____

3. Use compatible numbers to estimate the quotient. Show your work.

   _____

4. Write the missing numbers in the division using the standard algorithm on the right.

   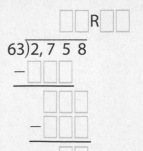

5. The class can buy _____ rabbits, and have $_____ left over.

6. Is this answer reasonable? Explain.

On the Back!

7. Divide. Check the answer by multiplying.

   $32\overline{)9,545}$

Tic Tac Toe

Get Started
 or

Get 20 squares in one color and 20 in another color. Get two number cubes for players to share. Get paper and a pencil. Take turns.

For Each Round

Toss one cube. That is the number of tens in a two-digit divisor. Toss the other cube. That is the number of ones in the same two-digit divisor. Explain how to divide 7,924 by that two-digit divisor. Cover the answer. If the answer is taken, lose your turn. Have fun!

Example

⚃ ⚄ ← **3** tens **5** ones

$$\begin{array}{r} 226 \text{ R}14 \\ 35\overline{)7{,}924} \\ -70 \\ \hline 92 \\ -70 \\ \hline 224 \\ -210 \\ \hline 14 \end{array}$$

Divide 7,924 by the two-digit divisor!

How to Win

The first player or team to cover a row, column, or diagonal in one of the four sections of the game board wins.

720 R4	146 R40	304 R20	127 R50	188 R28	121 R59
123 R52	330 R4	172 R12	344 R12	566	144 R4
495 R4	226 R14	660 R4	233 R2	120 R4	180 R4
184 R12	255 R19	193 R11	155 R19	141 R28	377 R7
149 R27	528 R4	176 R4	152 R20	609 R7	247 R20
240 R4	129 R55	360 R4	316 R24	125 R49	220 R4

If you have more time Play again!

Tic Tac Toe

Get Started 👥 or 👥👥
Get 20 squares in one color and 20 in another color. Get two number cubes for players to share. Get paper and a pencil. Take turns.

For Each Round
Toss two cubes. Make either number the number of tens in a two-digit divisor. Make the other number the number of ones in the same two-digit divisor. Find the dividend and the quotient with that number as the missing divisor. Explain your answer. Cover the answer. If the answer is taken, lose your turn. Have fun!

Find the missing divisor!

Example
🎲🎲 **3** tens **5** ones **or 5** tens **3** ones
Choose a divisor of **35** or **53**.
Use estimation to help you place that divisor below. Multiply to check.

How to Win
The first player or team to cover a row, column, or diagonal in one of the four sections of the game board wins.

14 R14 ☐ ☐)924	71 R1 ☐ ☐)924	15 R9 ☐ ☐)924	66 ☐ ☐)924	17 R6 ☐ ☐)924	20 R4 ☐ ☐)924
14 ☐ ☐)924	16 R28 ☐ ☐)924	35 R14 ☐ ☐)924	27 R6 ☐ ☐)924	17 R23 ☐ ☐)924	38 R12 ☐ ☐)924
14 R56 ☐ ☐)924	21 R21 ☐ ☐)924	14 R28 ☐ ☐)924	44 ☐ ☐)924	17 R40 ☐ ☐)924	21 ☐ ☐)924
42 ☐ ☐)924	14 R42 ☐ ☐)924	29 R25 ☐ ☐)924	84 ☐ ☐)924	57 R12 ☐ ☐)924	26 R14 ☐ ☐)924
20 R24 ☐ ☐)924	77 ☐ ☐)924	22 R22 ☐ ☐)924	61 R9 ☐ ☐)924	25 R24 ☐ ☐)924	36 R24 ☐ ☐)924
16 R44 ☐ ☐)924	28 ☐ ☐)924	18 R6 ☐ ☐)924	28 R28 ☐ ☐)924	22 ☐ ☐)924	40 R4 ☐ ☐)924

If you have more time 🕐 Play again!

Name _____

1. Brad used the compatible numbers 810 ÷ 90 for an estimate. Which quotient might he be finding?

   (A) 5380 ÷ 59

   (B) 822 ÷ 91

   (C) 277 ÷ 31

   (D) 84 ÷ 9

2. Divide.

   $27\overline{)12{,}562}$

   (A) 464 R20

   (B) 465

   (C) 465 R7

   (D) 4,657

3. Which equation best represents the data in the table?

r	0	3	6	9
s	0	2	4	6

   (A) $s = r + 4$

   (B) $s = 3r$

   (C) $s = \frac{1}{3}r$

   (D) $s = \frac{2}{3}r$

4. Which value, if any, from the set below is the solution of the equation $68.4 - d = 43.9$?

   23.5, 25.5, 112.3

   (A) 23.5

   (B) 25.5

   (C) 112.3

   (D) No solution is given in the set of values.

Amber went on a bike ride in a forest preserve. She rode at a constant rate of 11.8 miles per hour.

5. Write an equation that describes the relationship between the time Amber biked, t (in hours), and the distance she covered, d (in miles).

   _____

6. How long would it take Amber to bike 35.4 miles?

   _____

7. A school orders 595 math textbooks. The books are shipped in cartons that hold 36 books each. What is the smallest number of cartons that can be used to ship the books?

   _____

8. On a map, Trevor's house is located at $(-4, 6)$ and the library is located at $(7, 6)$. Each unit on the map is 1 mile. How many miles is Trevor's house from the library?

   _____

9. After 1 hour, Ina completed 35 items, or $\frac{7}{11}$ of all the items on her math test. Use the equation $\frac{7}{11}k = 35$ to find the total number of items on the test, k.

   _____

Name _____

Vocabulary

1. **Division** is a mathematical operation that can help answer two types of questions. First, if a quantity is separated into groups of a certain size, how many groups will there be? Second, if a quantity is separated into a certain number of equal-sized groups, how many items will be in each group?

   Write a division expression for each situation. Then answer each question.

   A box of gum is separated into packs of 7 sticks. If there are 70 sticks of gum in the box, how many packs are there? _____

   Maddie has 12 cups of flour. She uses all of the flour to make 6 batches of a recipe. How many cups of flour were used in each batch? _____

2. Over the course of 12 home games, a high school basketball team had a total attendance of 2,844 fans.

   Write an expression that can be used to represent the number of fans that attended each game, on average.

   _____

3. Use compatible numbers to estimate the solution. Show your work.

   _____

   _____

4. Since the quotient is about _____, the first digit of the quotient should be in the _____ place.

5. Write the missing numbers in the division using the standard algorithm on the right.

6. On average, _____ fans attended each home game.

$$12\overline{)2,8\ 4\ 4}$$

On the Back!

7. Estimate first. Then find the quotient.

   $$59\overline{)46,083}$$

Quick Questions

Partner Talk

Share your thinking while you work.

Get Started
♟ or ♟♟♟ or ♟♟♟

Each player tosses two number cubes. If your numbers match another player's numbers, toss again.
Decide who will read the first question. Take turns.

For Each Question

Listen to the reader. Discuss and agree on an estimate. Ask one student to find the quotient. That student rounds the quotient to the nearest whole number if necessary, and then reads the quotient. Every player who has the digit in the hundreds place in the quotient can remove <u>one</u> cube that shows the answer.

How to Win

The first player who removes both cubes wins. Have fun!

a	Divide 6,591 by 42. The quotient has which digit in the hundreds place?
b	Divide 8,825 by 14. The quotient has which digit in the hundreds place?
c	Divide 9,161 by 81. The quotient has which digit in the hundreds place?
d	Divide 8,626 by 27. The quotient has which digit in the hundreds place?
e	Divide 5,637 by 11. The quotient has which digit in the hundreds place?
f	Divide 8,966 by 36. The quotient has which digit in the hundreds place?
g	Divide 8,418 by 18. The quotient has which digit in the hundreds place?
h	Divide 9,959 by 23. The quotient has which digit in the hundreds place?
i	Divide 6,693 by 23. The quotient has which digit in the hundreds place?
j	Divide 8,168 by 16. The quotient has which digit in the hundreds place?
k	Divide 7,979 by 39. The quotient has which digit in the hundreds place?
l	Divide 9,651 by 16. The quotient has which digit in the hundreds place?
m	Divide 9,389 by 24. The quotient has which digit in the hundreds place?

n	Divide 9,547 by 29. The quotient has which digit in the hundreds place?
o	Divide 7,040 by 16. The quotient has which digit in the hundreds place?
p	Divide 8,773 by 68. The quotient has which digit in the hundreds place?
q	Divide 6,318 by 12. The quotient has which digit in the hundreds place?
r	Divide 5,222 by 14. The quotient has which digit in the hundreds place?
s	Divide 9,345 by 15. The quotient has which digit in the hundreds place?
t	Divide 8,458 by 72. The quotient has which digit in the hundreds place?
u	Divide 5,980 by 14. The quotient has which digit in the hundreds place?
v	Divide 7,594 by 37. The quotient has which digit in the hundreds place?
w	Divide 4,346 by 12. The quotient has which digit in the hundreds place?
x	Divide 7,723 by 13. The quotient has which digit in the hundreds place?
y	Divide 8,895 by 14. The quotient has which digit in the hundreds place?
z	Divide 5,797 by 25. The quotient has which digit in the hundreds place?

If you have more time

Toss two number cubes again. Play another game.
Begin with the next question in the list.

Center Game ★ 6•3

Quick Questions

Get Started or or

Each player tosses two number cubes. If your numbers match another player's numbers, toss again. Decide who will read the first question. Take turns.

For Each Question

Listen to the reader. Discuss and agree on an estimate. Ask one student to find the quotient. That student rounds the quotient to the nearest whole number and then reads the quotient. Every player who has the digit in the ones place in the quotient can remove <u>one</u> cube that shows the answer.

How to Win

The first player who removes both cubes wins. Have fun!

a	Divide 2,891 by 68. The quotient has which digit in the ones place?		n	Divide 7,780 by 76. The quotient has which digit in the ones place?
b	Divide 9,027 by 49. The quotient has which digit in the ones place?		o	Divide 8,195 by 34. The quotient has which digit in the ones place?
c	Divide 1,378 by 39. The quotient has which digit in the ones place?		p	Divide 6,505 by 49. The quotient has which digit in the ones place?
d	Divide 5,917 by 53. The quotient has which digit in the ones place?		q	Divide 8,163 by 22. The quotient has which digit in the ones place?
e	Divide 4,349 by 77. The quotient has which digit in the ones place?		r	Divide 6,566 by 62. The quotient has which digit in the ones place?
f	Divide 4,038 by 47. The quotient has which digit in the ones place?		s	Divide 2,059 by 60. The quotient has which digit in the ones place?
g	Divide 2,770 by 63. The quotient has which digit in the ones place?		t	Divide 8,340 by 99. The quotient has which digit in the ones place?
h	Divide 8,236 by 68. The quotient has which digit in the ones place?		u	Divide 9,053 by 64. The quotient has which digit in the ones place?
i	Divide 3,691 by 87. The quotient has which digit in the ones place?		v	Divide 5,438 by 59. The quotient has which digit in the ones place?
j	Divide 9,957 by 95. The quotient has which digit in the ones place?		w	Divide 3,802 by 51. The quotient has which digit in the ones place?
k	Divide 7,268 by 97. The quotient has which digit in the ones place?		x	Divide 6,154 by 97. The quotient has which digit in the ones place?
l	Divide 4,747 by 55. The quotient has which digit in the ones place?		y	Divide 2,891 by 67. The quotient has which digit in the ones place?
m	Divide 1,651 by 30. The quotient has which digit in the ones place?		z	Divide 7,077 by 97. The quotient has which digit in the ones place?

If you have more time Play another game. Begin with the next question in the list. Or make up your own questions like these. Play the game with your questions.

Center Game ★★ 6•3

1. Select all the statements that are true for $23\overline{)1{,}044}$.

   ☐ The quotient is about 50.

   ☐ The quotient is about 500.

   ☐ The remainder is 19.

   ☐ The remainder is 9.

   ☐ The quotient is between 43 and 48.

2. A school auditorium has 1,008 seats in 42 equal rows. How many seats are in each row?

   Ⓐ 23

   Ⓑ 24

   Ⓒ 42

   Ⓓ 43

3. Point P has a positive x-coordinate and a negative y-coordinate. In which quadrant is point P located?

   Ⓐ Quadrant I

   Ⓑ Quadrant II

   Ⓒ Quadrant III

   Ⓓ Quadrant IV

4. Melanie graphed point $T(2, -4)$ and point $U(-7, -4)$ on a coordinate plane. What is the distance between point T and point U?

   Ⓐ 13 units

   Ⓑ 9 units

   Ⓒ 5 units

   Ⓓ 3 units

5. A point is reflected over the y-axis to graph a new point. Are the x-coordinates or the y-coordinates of these points opposite each other?

   _____

6. Plot point $A\left(-1\frac{1}{3}, 2\frac{2}{3}\right)$ on the coordinate plane.

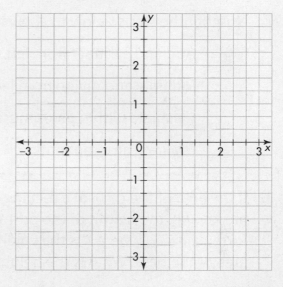

7. Explain how to solve $\frac{w}{26} = 35$. Then solve.

   _____

   _____

8. The area of a rectangular city park is 16,150 square feet. If the park is 95 feet wide, what is its length?

   _____

9. What is the coefficient of b in the expression $2.75a + 5.83b - 6.29$?

   _____

Name _____

Vocabulary

1. A **formula** is a rule that uses symbols to relate two or more quantities.

   Use variables to complete the formula.

   The width, *w*, of a rectangle is equal to its area, *a*, divided by its height, *h*.

   $w = \dfrac{\square}{\square}$

2. The **order of operations** are a set of rules that determine the order in which operations are performed. These rules should be followed when evaluating expressions.

   Number the steps below to show the correct order of operations.

   _____ Add and subtract from left to right.

   _____ Multiply and divide from left to right.

   _____ Calculate within parentheses.

   _____ Evaluate all exponents.

3. If the area of the base of a rectangular prism and its volume are known, the height of the prism, *h*, can be found using the formula $h = \dfrac{V}{B}$, where *V* is the volume of the prism and *B* is the area of the base. What is the height of the prism shown?

   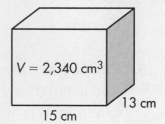

   V = 2,340 cm³
   13 cm
   15 cm

   Identify the values of the variables *V* and *B*.

   $V =$ _____

   $B =$ _____ × _____ = _____

4. Substitute the values of the variables into the formula and evaluate.

   So, the height of the prism is _____ cm.

   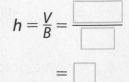

   $h = \dfrac{V}{B} = \dfrac{\square}{\square}$

   $= \square$

On the Back!

5. Evaluate the expression for *x* = 2, *x* = 9, and *x* = 16.

   $$\dfrac{1{,}584 + 144x}{4}$$

Name _____

1. What is the value of the expression when $z = 7$?

$$47 + \frac{480}{8 + z}$$

(A) 32

(B) $35\frac{2}{15}$

(C) 79

(D) 89

2. Milo correctly divided 35,876 by 42. What quotient did he get?

(A) 854

(B) 854 R2

(C) 854 R8

(D) 854 R18

3. The table shows Lin's age and Yi's age. Which expression can be used to find Yi's age if Lin is x years old?

Lin	4	8	12	x
Yi	1	5	9	

(A) $x - 3$

(B) $\frac{x}{4}$

(C) $4x$

(D) $x + 3$

4. Which inequality is **NOT** true?

(A) $-\frac{7}{8} < -\frac{1}{2}$

(B) $6.98 > 6.89$

(C) $-3\frac{7}{8} > -3\frac{5}{6}$

(D) $-0.001 < 0$

5. Evaluate the expression for the values of x.

x	2	6	10	14
$\frac{250 - 15x}{4}$				

6. Which person's account balance shows a debt greater than $225?

Account	Balance ($)
Alyssa	88
Ben	−185
Carrie	−232
Derek	396

7. The formula $m = \frac{d}{g}$ can be used to calculate gas mileage, m, in miles per gallon, where g is the number of gallons used to travel a distance of d miles. Rachel's car used 15 gallons to travel 495 miles. What is the gas mileage for this trip?

_____

8. Student tickets for a school play cost $16 each. The drama club made $1,344 on student ticket sales. How many student tickets were purchased?

_____

Name _____

ⒶⓏ Vocabulary

1. A **variable** is a letter or symbol, such as *n*, that represents an unknown number. To solve an equation, find the value of the variable that makes the equation true.

Solve each equation. The first one is done for you.

$7n = 63$
$n = 9$

$320 \div 10 = y$
$y = \square$

$\frac{16}{2} = z$
$z = \square$

$\frac{63}{n} = 7$
$n = \square$

$10y = 320$
$y = \square$

$\frac{16}{z} = 2$
$z = \square$

2. A load of mulch weighs 2,241 pounds. Jack can carry 83 pounds of mulch at a time in a wheelbarrow. How many wheelbarrows full of mulch, *w*, will it take for Jack to move the entire load?

Write a multiplication equation and a division equation to represent the problem.

Multiplication equation   **Division equation**

_____   _____

3. Divide to find the number of wheelbarrows of mulch.

4. Use multiplication to check the division. Does your answer check?

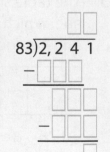

_____

5. Jack will take _____ wheelbarrows full of mulch to move the entire load.

On the Back!

6. Shanika drives 567 miles in 9 hours. Suppose she drives the same speed, *s*, throughout her trip. Write and solve an equation to find the speed at which Shanika drives.

Name _____

1. Which equation has a solution of $x = 24$? Select all that apply.

☐ $2,352 \div 98 = x$

☐ $3,780 \div x = 135$

☐ $4,536 \div x = 189$

☐ $19,918 \div x = 866$

☐ $92x = 2,208$

2. What is the value of the expression when $r = 12$?

$$\frac{230 + r}{11}$$

Ⓐ 21   Ⓒ 23

Ⓑ 22   Ⓓ 24

3. Madeline earns $13 per hour. Last month, she earned $1,586. Which equation CANNOT be used to find h, the number of hours Madeline worked last month?

Ⓐ $1,586 \times 13 = h$

Ⓑ $1,586 \div h = 13$

Ⓒ $\frac{1,586}{13} = h$

Ⓓ $h = 1,586 \div 13$

4. Canned soups are shipped to a grocery store in crates that hold up to 48 cans each. A grocery store orders 1,650 cans of soup. What is the smallest number of crates possible for the shipment?

Ⓐ 33 crates

Ⓑ 34 crates

Ⓒ 35 crates

Ⓓ 36 crates

5. Complete the table for the equation $y = \frac{x}{2} - 1$.

x	y
2	
4	
6	
8	

6. Use the data in the table from Exercise 5 to graph the equation $y = \frac{x}{2} - 1$.

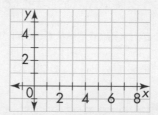

7. Solve.

$9,635 = 47n$

_____

8. A parking lot has 1,035 parking spaces with 23 spaces in each row. How many rows are there in the parking lot?

_____

_____

Name _____

A-Z Vocabulary

1. In mathematics, a **table** is often used to organize data. Column headings are used to describe the data.

Fill in the table to organize the data given in this situation.

A baker is packing gourmet granola into gift bags. Small and large bags hold 2 pounds and 10 pounds of granola. The prices of the bags of granola are $28 and $110.

Gourmet Granola		
Bag Size	**Weight**	_____
Small	2 pounds	
		$110

2. Mrs. Ferguson needs 360 pounds of clay for an art project. The store sells 3 different-sized boxes of clay: small: 25 pounds for $24.88, medium: 50 pounds for $48.00, and large: 75 pounds for $70.00. Mrs. Ferguson already has 1 box of each size.

How many pounds of clay does Mrs. Ferguson need to buy?

She already has _____ pounds. She needs _____ pounds.

3. Fill in the table to compare costs of clay.

4. What is the least expensive combination of boxes of clay that Mrs. Ferguson can buy so that she has exactly enough clay for her project? Divide to find the number of large boxes needed.

Pounds of Clay	Box Description	Cost
150	_____ large	$140.00
150	3 medium	_____
150	_____ small	$149.28

$210 \div$ _____ $=$ _____ R _____

5. So, Mrs. Ferguson should buy _____ large box(es), _____ medium box(es), and _____ small box(es).

On the Back!

6. An average of 2,900 commuters use a train system each weekday. The transit authority estimates that in 5 years, the number of commuters will increase by $\frac{4}{9}$. Each train in the system can carry up to 300 passengers per day. How many trains will the system need in 5 years?

Fluently Add, Subtract, Multiply, and Divide Decimals

Topic 7 Standards
6.NS.B.2, 6.NS.B.3, 6.EE.A.2a, 6.EE.A.2c, 6.EE.B.7
See the front of the Student's Edition for complete standards.

Dear Family,

Your child is learning how to estimate with decimals and how to use estimation to check that his or her answers are reasonable. Your child will learn how to add, subtract, multiply and divide decimals, and how to evaluate expressions with decimals and find solutions to decimal equations.

Here is an activity you can do with your child to help him or her develop estimation skills.

Rolling Decimals

Materials number cube

Step 1 Roll a number cube six times. Write two three-digit numbers using the digits you rolled. Insert a decimal point in both numbers. For example, you might write 23.6 and 0.125.

Step 2 Write an equation for each of the operations using the two numbers. Estimate the answers to the equations. Compare the results with your estimations.

Step 3 After you and your child take turns making up numbers and estimating the results of different operations, choose an estimation goal, such as 100 or 25.5. Challenge your child to write equations with decimals that will come as close to the estimate as possible.

Observe Your Child

Focus on Mathematical Practice 2
Reason abstractly and quantitatively.

Help your child become proficient with Mathematical Practice 2. Be sure to have your child write or record all estimates for computations with decimals. Solving the computations and comparing the results with the estimates confirms your child's ability to reason abstractly and quantitatively.

Sumar, restar, multiplicar y dividir números decimales con facilidad

Estándares del Tema 7

6.SN.B.2, 6.SN.B.3, 6.EE.A.2a, 6.EE.A.2c, 6.EE.B.7

Los estándares completos se encuentran en las páginas preliminares del Libro del estudiante.

Estimada familia:

Su niño(a) está aprendiendo a estimar con números decimales y a usar la estimación para comprobar que las respuestas sean razonables. Aprenderá a sumar, restar, multiplicar y dividir números decimales; a evaluar expresiones con números decimales y a encontrar soluciones de ecuaciones con decimales.

Esta es una actividad que puede realizar con su niño(a) para desarrollar sus destrezas de estimación.

Lanzar números decimales

Materiales cubo numérico

Paso 1 Lancen un cubo numérico seis veces. Escriban dos números de tres dígitos usando los dígitos que salieron en el lanzamiento. Agreguen un punto decimal en ambos números. Por ejemplo, se puede escribir 23.6 y 0.125.

Paso 2 Escriban una ecuación para cada una de las operaciones usando los dos números. Estimen las respuestas a las ecuaciones. Comparen los resultados con las estimaciones.

Paso 3 Luego de que usted y su niño(a) se turnen para formar números y estimar los resultados de diferentes operaciones, escojan un objetivo de estimación, como 100 o 25.5. Anime a su niño(a) a escribir ecuaciones con números decimales que tengan como resultado un número lo más cerca posible de la estimación.

Observe a su niño(a)

Enfoque en la Práctica matemática 2
Razonar de manera abstracta y cuantitativa.

Ayude a su niño(a) a adquirir competencia en la Práctica matemática 2. Asegúrese de que su niño(a) anote todas las estimaciones de los cálculos con números decimales. Resolver los cálculos y comparar los resultados con las estimaciones confirma la capacidad de su niño(a) de razonar de manera abstracta y cuantitativa.

Name _____

Fluently Add, Subtract, Multiply, and Divide Multi-Digit Decimals

1.   1.56
   + 672.3

2.   43.613
   + 224.73

3.   52.6
   + 2.5

4.   0.286
   + 55.057

5.   17.7
   − 7.94

6.   58.156
   − 0.180

7.   16.373
   − 0.859

8.   75.234
   − 52.5

9.   72.83
   × 8.6

10.   4.9
   × 5.6

11.   7.23
   × 0.55

12.   4.62
   × 98.9

13. $8.49\overline{)71.316}$

14. $0.7\overline{)5.32}$

15. $5.8\overline{)295.626}$

16. $9.9\overline{)11.88}$

17. For the first three weeks of the month, a bakery had $5,108.16 in sales. During the fourth week, sales were $1,145.73. What were the total sales for the month? Show your work.

Fluently Add, Subtract, Multiply, and Divide Multi-Digit Decimals

1. 64.9
    + 72.07

2. 9.048
    + 9.93

3. 26.3
    + 1.8

4. 235.80
    + 285.24

5. 384.41
    − 9.5

6. 88.52
    − 1.50

7. 135.890
    − 98.831

8. 669.76
    − 89.413

9. 901.59
    × 3.3

10. 398.7
    × 16.9

11. 102.7
    × 6.17

12. 16.92
    × 77.6

13. 7.52)221.84

14. 0.8)49.44

15. 55.9)181.675

16. 6.45)54.825

17. Insert one digit in each box to complete the subtraction problem. You will not use the same digit twice.

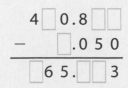

Fluently Add, Subtract, Multiply, and Divide Multi-Digit Decimals

1. 883.10
+ 9.09

2. 5.742
+ 49.528

3. 3.74
+ 931.1

4. 90.2
+ 142.285

5. 53.35
− 9.1

6. 73.670
− 5.797

7. 41.2
− 27.228

8. 87.502
− 3.782

9. 236.2
× 48.3

10. 95.96
× 5.8

11. 95.44
× 5.89

12. 36.91
× 36.8

13. 8.1)416.34

14. 2.2)0.836

15. 5.5)254.65

16. 5.64)50.76

17. Two decimal numbers are multiplied. None of the digits in either factor or the product are zero. One of the factors has three digits to the right of the decimal point. The product has four digits to the right of the decimal point. How many digits are to the right of the decimal point in the second factor? Explain your answer.

Fluently Add, Subtract, Multiply, and Divide Multi-Digit Decimals

1.   3.125
    $+\,86.62$

2.   1.45
    $+\,519.832$

3. 650.9
    $+\,4.4$

4.   54.437
    $+\,37.816$

5.   733.721
    $-\,359.66$

6.   3.8
    $-\,2.13$

7.   536.7
    $-\,161.475$

8.   75.44
    $-\,51.70$

9.   79.96
    $\times\,1.42$

10.   59.26
    $\times\,0.7$

11.   7.76
    $\times\,5.72$

12.   32.9
    $\times\,1.03$

13. $0.12\overline{)84.9}$

14. $0.827\overline{)80.7152}$

15. $19\overline{)136.04}$

16. $0.84\overline{)11.592}$

17. A rectangular sheet of paper has an area of 96.25 square inches. The paper is 11 inches long. What is the width of the paper? Show your work.

Fluently Add, Subtract, Multiply, and Divide Multi-Digit Decimals

1. $\begin{array}{r} 5.22 \\ + 23.22 \\ \hline \end{array}$

2. $\begin{array}{r} 6.8 \\ + 89.958 \\ \hline \end{array}$

3. $\begin{array}{r} 906.077 \\ + 813.2 \\ \hline \end{array}$

4. $\begin{array}{r} 131.400 \\ + 6.414 \\ \hline \end{array}$

5. $\begin{array}{r} 62.5 \\ - 7.857 \\ \hline \end{array}$

6. $\begin{array}{r} 4.57 \\ - 4.30 \\ \hline \end{array}$

7. $\begin{array}{r} 70.6 \\ - 35.64 \\ \hline \end{array}$

8. $\begin{array}{r} 99.089 \\ - 1.77 \\ \hline \end{array}$

9. $\begin{array}{r} 24.02 \\ \times\ 6.53 \\ \hline \end{array}$

10. $\begin{array}{r} 70.56 \\ \times\ 0.49 \\ \hline \end{array}$

11. $\begin{array}{r} 691.1 \\ \times\ 12.4 \\ \hline \end{array}$

12. $\begin{array}{r} 62.75 \\ \times\ 9.42 \\ \hline \end{array}$

13. $8.5\overline{)1.0795}$

14. $8.3\overline{)744.51}$

15. $0.72\overline{)457.56}$

16. $3.7\overline{)0.4699}$

---

17. The quotient of $72.644 \div 2.54 = 28.6$. Without calculating, what is the product of 28.6 and 2.54? Explain how you know.

Name _____

Fluently Add, Subtract, Multiply, and Divide Multi-Digit Decimals

1. 49.3
    + 29.734

2. 9.76
    + 1.9

3. 42.6
    + 4.287

4. 4.71
    + 42.56

5. 313.2
    − 2.8

6. 851.709
    − 11.607

7. 333.6
    − 9.059

8. 425.9
    − 31.71

9. 70.24
    × 2.52

10. 52.72
    × 0.95

11. 642.4
    × 2.4

12. 75.5
    × 0.95

13. $23\overline{)103.27}$

14. $2.3\overline{)112.24}$

15. $0.292\overline{)5.4896}$

16. $5.9\overline{)0.5723}$

....

17. Bianca weighs 46.72 kilograms. Oscar weighs 73.482 kilograms. How much more does Oscar weigh than Bianca? Show your work.

Name _____

Mass Conservation

Did You Know? Matter is a general term for the objects around us. Matter occupies space and has mass. Spiders, rocks, air, apples, and you are all examples of matter. The law of conservation of mass states that matter can be neither created nor destroyed. This means that in an ordinary chemical reaction, the sum of the masses of the reactants (the substances undergoing change) equals the sum of the masses of the products.

Law of Conservation of Mass

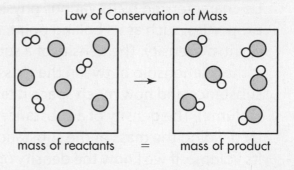

mass of reactants = mass of product

1 When hydrogen (H) combines with oxygen (O) to form water (H_2O), a chemical reaction takes place. Hydrogen and oxygen are the reactants and water is the product. Suppose 4.032 grams of hydrogen combine with 31.998 grams of oxygen. According to the law of conservation of mass, how many grams of water does the reaction produce?

2 **Represent** Hydrochloric acid (HCl) reacts with sodium hydroxide (NaOH) to form sodium chloride (NaCl) and water (H_2O). The equation below represents the reaction.

36.461 g (HCl) + ⬚ g (NaOH) = 58.442 g (NaCl) + 18.015 g (H_2O)

How many grams of NaOH are required to react with HCl to form the products?

3 **Extension** Suppose 2 carbon (C) atoms react with 2 oxygen (O) atoms to form 2 molecules of carbon monoxide (CO). One molecule of carbon monoxide is made up of 1 atom of carbon and 1 atom of oxygen. The mass of 1 carbon atom is 12.010 atomic mass units and the mass of 1 oxygen atom is 15.999 atomic mass units.

What is the mass of 1 molecule of carbon monoxide?

Name _____

Density

Did You Know? A pure substance can be characterized by its various physical properties, such as its boiling point, freezing point, or density. The density of a substance is the relationship between the mass of the substance and how much space it takes up (volume). The density of a substance is found by dividing the mass of the substance by its volume. If we know the density of a pure substance, we can identify the substance.

Densities of Common Substances
(grams per cubic centimeter $= \frac{g}{cm^3}$)

Water	1
Silver	10.49
Gold	19.3
Platinum	21.09
Lead	11.34
Iron	7.874
Copper	8.92
Titanium	4.507

$$density = \frac{mass}{volume} \quad volume = \frac{mass}{density}$$

$$mass = density \times volume$$

1 A metal sample has a mass of 28.544 grams and a volume of 3.2 cm³. Which metal could this sample be?

_____

2 Liam determines the mass of a pure silver coin to be 68.185 grams. How many cubic centimeters of silver were used to make the coin?

_____

3 **Extension** King Hiero of Syracuse, who reigned from 270 to 215 BC, commissioned a new crown to be made of pure gold. King Hiero provided the goldsmith with the gold to make the crown. When the crown was delivered, King Hiero suspected that the goldsmith added some other metal to the gold so that he could keep some of the gold for himself and still have enough metal to make the crown. The crown had a mass of 998.58 grams and a volume of 53.4 cm³. Did the goldsmith cheat the king? Justify your answer.

_____

_____

_____

_____

Math and Science Activity   **7·7**   **6**

1. Which of these numbers falls between 7.073 and 7.082 on a number line?

Ⓐ 7.02

Ⓑ 7.064

Ⓒ 7.072

Ⓓ 7.08

2. Divide.

$67\overline{)58{,}923}$

Ⓐ 879

Ⓑ 879 R2

Ⓒ 879 R30

Ⓓ 879 R33

3. Which ordered pair represents the reflection of the point $P(-4.5, 9.7)$ across both axes?

Ⓐ (4.5, 9.7)

Ⓑ (4.5, −9.7)

Ⓒ (−4.5, −9.7)

Ⓓ (9.7, −4.5)

4. Ben earns $14 per hour. In April, he earned $1,932. Which equation could **NOT** be used to find h, the number of hours Ben worked in April?

Ⓐ $1{,}932 \div h = 14$

Ⓑ $\frac{1{,}932}{14} = h$

Ⓒ $1{,}932 \times 14 = h$

Ⓓ $14 \times h = 1{,}932$

5. Evaluate the expression for the values of x.

x	0	5	10	15
$\dfrac{180 - 12x}{5}$				

6. The formula $m = \frac{d}{g}$ can be used to calculate gas mileage in miles per gallon, where g is the number of gallons used to travel a distance of d miles. Use the formula to find Rita's gas mileage if she used 14 gallons to travel 504 miles.

_____

Steve and Sara went on a hike in a state park. They hiked at a constant rate of 3.2 miles per hour.

7. Write an equation that describes the relationship between the time Steve and Sara hiked, t (in hours), and the distance they covered, d (in miles).

_____

8. How long would it take Steve and Sara to hike 12.8 miles?

_____

9. Solve the equation.

$\frac{9}{13}z = 54$

_____

D 7·1

Name _____

🅰🇿 Vocabulary ─────────────────────────────────

1. To **estimate** means to find an answer close to the exact answer. An estimate is approximately equal to (≈) the exact answer. You can use **rounding** or **compatible numbers** to estimate.

   Is the answer exact or an estimate?

   $24.7 - 21.2 = 3.5$ _____ $3.4 + 1.5 = 4.9$ _____

   $24.7 - 21.2 ≈ 4$ _____ $3.4 + 1.5 ≈ 5$ _____

2. You can apply the same strategies for rounding whole numbers to rounding decimal numbers. Round each decimal number to the nearest whole number.

   5.6 rounds up to _____ because the digit to the right of the decimal point is greater than or equal to 5.

   7.4 rounds down to _____ because the digit to the right of the decimal point is less than 5.

3. Use the digit to the right of the decimal point to round each decimal number to the nearest whole number.

   $9.\mathbf{7}4 ≈$ _____

   $14.\mathbf{0}59 ≈$ _____

4. Use the rounded numbers from Exercise 3 to estimate the difference $14.059 - 9.74$.

   $14.059 - 9.74 ≈$ _____ $-$ _____

   So, $14.059 - 9.74 ≈$ _____

5. Use compatible numbers to the tenths place to estimate the difference $12.4 - 6.32$.

   $12.4 - 6.32 ≈ 12.4 -$ _____ $≈$ _____

On the Back!

6. Round to the nearest whole number to estimate $5.78 + 8.315$.

Think Together

Partner Talk

Share your thinking while you work.

Get Started 👥 or 👥👥

Put 1 2 3 4 in a bag.

For Each Round

Choose **A, B, C, D, E,** or **F.** Ask someone to read the directions aloud.
Pick a tile. Pick two tiles if your group has only two students.
Estimate the expression next to your number when it is your turn.
Discuss: How can you use mental math to make your estimate?

A Round to the nearest whole number to estimate each sum.

1	42.58 + 9.14
2	1.67 + 13.21
3	4.75 + 19.4
4	26.1 + 11.4

B Round to the nearest whole number to estimate each difference.

1	16.7 − 8.2
2	45.4 − 19.7
3	9.27 − 4.45
4	325.1 − 44.8

C Round to the nearest whole number to estimate each sum.

1	9.54 + 8.02
2	56.7 + 28.9
3	8.61 + 9.73
4	41.51 + 37.2

D Round to the nearest whole number to estimate each difference.

1	49.6 − 22.3
2	64.1 − 26.3
3	9.58 − 3.61
4	32.7 − 5.21

E Round to the nearest whole number to estimate each sum.

1	19.4 + 18.6
2	82.7 + 39.2
3	71.4 + 28.8
4	29.5 + 29.4

F Round to the nearest whole number to estimate each difference.

1	26.3 − 15.8
2	42.7 − 5.9
3	7.64 − 1.23
4	19.2 − 9.81

If you have more time Make up a set of "Think Together" expressions for your group to practice estimating to the nearest whole number. Ask your classmates to estimate the sums or differences for your expressions.

Center Game ★ 7·1

Think Together

Partner Talk

Share your thinking while you work.

Get Started  **or**

Put [1] [2] [3] [4] in a bag.

For Each Round

Choose A, B, C, D, E, or F. Ask someone to read the question aloud.
Pick a tile. Pick two tiles if your group has only two students.
Estimate the expression next to your number when it is your turn.
Discuss: How can you use mental math to make your estimate?
Decide: Are you likely to get closer to the exact sum or difference when you round to the nearest whole number, or when you round to the nearest tenth? Why?

A — Round to the nearest tenth to estimate each sum.

[1]	2.75 + 8.14
[2]	14.31 + 9.43
[3]	50.15 + 19.28
[4]	7.145 + 13.94

B — Round to the nearest tenth to estimate each difference.

[1]	16.54 − 9.27
[2]	4.86 − 1.97
[3]	47.03 − 21.58
[4]	19.27 − 10.41

C — Round to the nearest tenth to estimate each sum.

[1]	5.261 + 4.812
[2]	27.21 + 13.48
[3]	6.047 + 9.074
[4]	53.86 + 27.75

D — Round to the nearest tenth to estimate each difference.

[1]	8.61 − 5.73
[2]	14.05 − 9.26
[3]	47.83 − 28.16
[4]	12.64 − 8.43

E — Round to the nearest tenth to estimate each sum.

[1]	48.61 + 8.06
[2]	14.53 + 19.27
[3]	52.16 + 21.58
[4]	19.43 + 8.77

F — Round to the nearest tenth to estimate each difference.

[1]	9.58 − 1.23
[2]	9.27 − 3.61
[3]	51.63 − 20.86
[4]	71.52 − 35.74

If you have more time

Make up a set of "Think Together" expressions for your group to practice estimating to the nearest tenth. Ask your classmates to estimate the sums or differences for your expressions.

Center Game ★★ 7·1

Name _____

1. Estimate the difference.

$436.78 - 239.41$

Ⓐ 40

Ⓑ 100

Ⓒ 200

Ⓓ 400

2. Which of these numbers would be located farthest to the right on a number line?

Ⓐ -5.45

Ⓑ $-\frac{6}{11}$

Ⓒ $-\frac{5}{9}$

Ⓓ -0.54

3. Rectangle *PQRS* has vertices $P(-6, 2)$, $Q(4, 2)$, $R(4, -5)$, and $S(-6, -5)$. What is its perimeter?

Ⓐ 28 units

Ⓑ 34 units

Ⓒ 36 units

Ⓓ 40 units

4. Which equation best represents the data in the table?

p	0	2	4	6
q	5	6	7	8

Ⓐ $q = 5 + p$

Ⓑ $q = 5 + \frac{p}{2}$

Ⓒ $q = 5 + \frac{p}{3}$

Ⓓ $q = 5 + 2p$

5. Victoria buys two of each of the items listed in the table.

Item	Price
Book	$28.95
Magazine	$4.75
Calendar	$9.20
Board game	$24.35

Estimate the total cost of the items she bought.

_____

6. A pharmacy warehouse packs 4,265 bottles of vitamins in cartons that hold 80 bottles each. How many cartons are needed to pack all of the bottles?

_____

The Jiménez family uses at least 150 gallons of water each day.

7. Write an inequality to represent the number of gallons of water, *g*, the Jiménez family uses each day.

_____

8. Label the number line below and graph the solution of the inequality you wrote in Exercise 7.

Name _____

⒜ Vocabulary

1. To **annex** means to add as an extra part.

    To annex a zero to a decimal means to _____ a zero to the right of the last
    digit in the decimal. Sometimes, you may have to write two or more _____.

2. When you annex a zero, the zero acts as a **placeholder**. Annex one
    or more zeros in the following addition or subtraction problems.

    $$\begin{array}{r} 1.45\_\_ \\ +\ 3.589 \end{array} \qquad \begin{array}{r} 27{,}779.7\_\_ \\ -\ 18{,}998.925 \end{array} \qquad \begin{array}{r} 4.1111 \\ +\ 0.6\_\_\_ \end{array}$$

3. It rained 1.8 inches on Tuesday and 0.24 inch on Wednesday.
    How many inches did it rain altogether?

    Write an expression you could use to solve this problem. Write a
    number or operation symbol in each box.

    ☐ ☐ ☐

4. Estimate the number of inches it rained altogether.

5. Rewrite the expression by lining up the decimal points vertically.

    The decimal 1.8 needs a placeholder in the _____ place.

    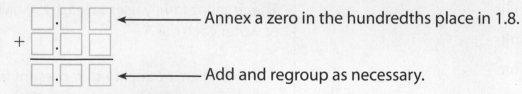
    ⟵ Annex a zero in the hundredths place in 1.8.

    ⟵ Add and regroup as necessary.

    It rained _____ inches altogether.

6. Is your answer reasonable? Explain.

    _____

    _____

On the Back!

7. Find the difference 15.25 − 7.14.

Name _____

1. Select all the expressions that have a sum or difference of 22.5.

   ☐ 9.8 + 12.7

   ☐ 3.5 + 18

   ☐ 39 − 16.5

   ☐ 43.1 − 20.6

   ☐ 62.8 − 41.3

2. A movie rental store rents DVDs for $2.50 each. The same store sells DVDs for $16.88 each. How much more does it cost to buy a DVD than to rent one?

   Ⓐ $19.38

   Ⓑ $18.38

   Ⓒ $16.38

   Ⓓ $14.38

3. The seating at a college basketball arena is divided into 18 sections. If the arena holds 16,812 spectators, what is the average number of seats in each section?

   Ⓐ 822

   Ⓑ 834

   Ⓒ 922

   Ⓓ 934

4. In which quadrant is the point (−5.8, 7.2) located?

   Ⓐ Quadrant I

   Ⓑ Quadrant II

   Ⓒ Quadrant III

   Ⓓ Quadrant IV

5. Graph and label each point on the coordinate plane below.

   $P(1.5, -1.25)$
   $Q(-0.75, 0)$
   $R(-1, -1.5)$
   $S(1.25, 1.75)$

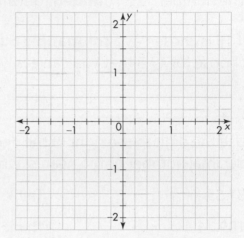

6. On a map, a school is located at (−7, −3) and a library is located at (−7, 6). If each unit on the map is a city block, how many blocks is the school from the library?

   _____

7. Molly buys one package of each party item listed in the table.

Item	Price Per Package
Favors	$4.85
Streamers	$2.99
Balloons	$9.38

   The sales tax on Molly's purchase is $0.86. If she pays with a $20 bill, how much change does she receive?

   _____

D 7·3

Name _____

Reteach to Build
Understanding
7-3

A-Z Vocabulary

1. When you multiply two or more numbers, the answer is called the **product**. You can use **rounding** or **compatible numbers** to estimate a product.

   Circle the expression that results in a product.

   $12.7 + 11.3$ 12.7×11.3 $12.7 \div 11.3$ $12.7 - 11.3$

2. The number 12.7 **rounded** to a whole number is _____.

3. If 15 is chosen as a **compatible number** for 12.7, what number could you choose for 11.3 that you can easily multiply (in your head) with 15?

   _____

4. Use the digit to the right of the decimal point to round each decimal number to the nearest whole number.

   $81.55 \approx$ _____   Think: _____ $\geq$ 5, so round 81.55 to _____.

   $109.24 \approx$ _____   Think: _____ $<$ 5, so round 109.24 to _____.

   $244.062 \approx$ _____   Think: _____ $<$ 5, so round 244.062 to _____.

   $1{,}372.999 \approx$ _____   Think: _____ $\geq$ 5, so round 1,372.999 to _____.

5. Use rounding to estimate the product 3.244×7.941. Round each number to the nearest whole number. Then multiply.

   3.244 rounds to _____, because _____ $<$ 5.

   7.941 rounds to _____, because 9 _____ 5.

   $3.244 \times 7.941 \approx$ _____ $\times$ _____   So, $3.244 \times 7.941 \approx$ _____.

6. Explain why you chose each compatible number. Use compatible numbers to estimate the product 45.59×8.46.

   $45.59 \times 8.46 \approx$ _____ $\times$ _____

   So, $45.59 \times 8.46 \approx$ _____

   _____

   _____

On the Back!

7. Estimate 2.76×6.23.

R 7·3

Copyright © Pearson Education, Inc., or its affiliates. All Rights Reserved. 6

Toss and Talk

Partner Talk

Share your thinking while you work.

Get Started  Get 10 squares in one color and 10 in another color.
Get two number cubes. Take turns with another player or team.
Talk about math as you play!

At Your Turn Toss two number cubes. Add the dots. Find your toss below.
Follow the directions. Explain your thinking. Cover the answer.
If the answer is taken, lose your turn. Have fun!

Toss	Explain how to use rounding to estimate each product.
2	32.4 × 9.8
3	21.1 × 9.3
4	152.8 × 3.2
5	29.7 × 7.9
6	47.8 × 10.4

7	1.83 × 16.4 × 4.71
8	5.41 × 2.35 × 16.78
9	19.76 × 21.32
10	29.5 × 6.7
11	52.341 × 4.925
12	17.6 × 9.7

150	300	400	500
180	170	240	160
160	200	210	250
240	400	170	450

How to Win You win if you are the first to get four connected rectangles, like:

If you have more time

Play again!

Center Game ★ 7-3

Toss and Talk

Partner Talk
Share your thinking while you work.

 **Get Started** 👥 or 👥👥
Get 10 squares in one color and 10 in another color.
Get two number cubes. Take turns with another player or team.
Talk about math as you play!

At Your Turn
Toss two number cubes. Add the dots. Find your toss below.
Follow the directions. Explain your thinking. Cover the answer.
If the answer is taken, lose your turn. Have fun!

Toss	Explain how to use compatible numbers to estimate each product.
2	39.7 × 4.8
3	4.23 × 149.6
4	41.8 × 7.94
5	25.64 × 7.2
6	31.1 × 11.2

7	21.2 × 5.27 × 3.86
8	7.16 × 7.93
9	2.35 × 0.61 × 4.04
10	6.127 × 0.79
11	96.4 × 3.18
12	17.13 × 5.78

8	320	56	100
6	400	330	300
120	600	5	8
330	175	400	200

How to Win
You win if you are the first to get four connected rectangles, like:

If you have more time
Play again!

Center Game ★★ **7·3**

Name _____

1. Round to the nearest tenth to estimate the sum.

$9.236 + 14.788$

Ⓐ 23.9

Ⓑ 24

Ⓒ 24.1

Ⓓ 24.2

2. A middle school has 286 sixth-graders participating in an all-school competition. There can be no more than 14 students on a team. What is the least possible number of sixth-grade teams?

Ⓐ 19 teams

Ⓑ 20 teams

Ⓒ 21 teams

Ⓓ 22 teams

3. Peaches are sold for $4.95 per basket at a local farm stand. On sale, peaches are sold for $3.99 per basket. How much do you save on the price per basket if you buy the peaches when they are on sale?

Ⓐ $1.16

Ⓑ $1.06

Ⓒ $1.04

Ⓓ $0.96

4. Complete the table for the equation $y = x + 0.5$.

x	y
0	
1	
2	
2.5	

5. Use the data from the table in Exercise 5 to graph the equation $y = x + 0.5$.

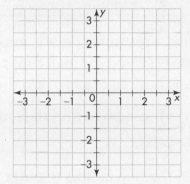

6. Pedro bought an ink cartridge and a smart phone case.

Item	Price
Ink cartridge	$29.95
Copy paper (1 ream)	$5.45
Smart phone case	$14.29
Digital camera battery	$18.50

Find the total cost of the items Pedro bought.

_____

Name _____

Vocabulary

1. **Place value** is important when multiplying decimals. The number 4.76 means 4 ones and 76 hundredths because the digits 4, 7, and 6 are in certain places. The number 2.6 means 2 ones and six tenths. You can apply place-value understanding to find the product of 4.76 and 2.6 using fractions or a general method.

$$4.76 \cdot 2.6 = \frac{476}{100} \cdot \frac{26}{10}$$

$$= \frac{12,376}{1,000}$$

4.76 ◄——— Number of decimal places: ____
✕ 2.6 ◄——— Number of decimal places: ____
2856
+ 9520
12 376 ◄——— The number of decimal places in the product is the sum of the decimal places in the factors: ____ + ____ = ____ .

Place the decimal point in the product.

2. The chef at a restaurant made enough sauce for 20.5 servings. The sauce is served in small cups that hold 3.275 ounces each. How many ounces of sauce did the chef make?

Write an expression to find the amount of sauce, in ounces, that the chef made. _____

First fill in the two factors in order to find the product.

Then multiply the decimals as if they were whole numbers.

☐.☐☐☐
✕ ☐☐.☐

How many decimal places are in 3.275? _____

How many decimal places are in 20.5? _____

How many decimal places are in the product? _____

Place the decimal point in the product.

How many ounces of sauce did the chef make? _____

On the Back!

3. Place the decimal point in the product.

3.4 ✕ 2.1 = 714

Tic Tac Toe

Partner Talk
Share your thinking while you work.

**Get Started** 👫 or 👫👤	Get 20 squares in one color and 20 in another color. Get paper and a pencil. Get two number cubes for players to share. Take turns.
For Each Round	Toss two cubes. Form a decimal by writing the two numbers with a decimal point between them. Form a second decimal by reversing the digits on either side of the decimal point. Explain how to multiply those decimals. If you toss a double, for example, 3 and 3, multiply 3.3 × 3.3. Cover the product. If the answer is taken, lose your turn.
Example	The decimals are **3.5** and **5.3**. Explain how to multiply **3.5 × 5.3**.
How to Win	The first player or team to cover a row, column, or diagonal in one of the four sections of the game board wins.

18.55	5.74	2.52	29.44	9.76	36.4
30.25	1.21	10.08	24.3	19.36	14.62
4.03	13	7.36	16.12	7.65	22.68
22.68	14.62	36.4	5.74	13	7.36
7.65	10.89	9.76	18.55	43.56	4.84
29.44	16.12	24.3	4.03	10.08	2.52

If you have more time Play again!

Tic Tac Toe

Get Started
Get 20 squares in one color and 20 in another color. Get paper and a pencil. Get two number cubes for players to share. Take turns.

For Each Round
Toss two cubes. Record the numbers you get, listing the lesser digit first. Create a decimal by placing a decimal point between the two digits. Form a second decimal by placing the decimal point to the left of both digits. Explain how to multiply the two decimals. If you toss a double, for example 3 and 3, multiply 3.3 × 0.33. Cover the product. If the answer is taken, lose your turn.

Example   The decimals are **3.5** and **0.35**. Explain how to multiply **3.5 × 0.35**.

How to Win
The first player or team to cover a row, column, or diagonal in one of the four sections of the game board wins.

1.024	0.676	3.136	0.441	4.225	2.809
3.969	1.936	0.576	1.681	1.089	0.529
0.256	1.156	0.169	3.844	2.601	2.025
0.961	2.916	3.721	0.484	0.196	0.144
4.096	0.121	0.225	1.225	4.356	0.625
1.849	1.764	3.025	2.116	2.704	1.296

If you have more time 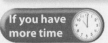 Play again!

Center Game ★★ **7·4**

1. Which describes how to find the number of decimal places in the product of two decimals?

   Ⓐ Add the decimal places in the factors.

   Ⓑ Subtract the decimal places in the factors.

   Ⓒ Multiply the decimal places in the factors.

   Ⓓ Divide the decimal places in the factors.

Use this table for Exercises **2** and **3**.

Summer sale

	Regular Price	Sale Price
Sunglasses	$15.79	$12.95
Flip-Flops	$8.78	$4.89
Swimsuits	$46.50	$24.59

2. At the sale, Nick bought 2 pairs of sunglasses. How much did he spend?

   Ⓐ $31.58

   Ⓑ $25.90

   Ⓒ $25.80

   Ⓓ $24.80

3. Lucy bought a pair of flip-flops and a swimsuit. How much money did she save by buying them on sale?

   Ⓐ $24.75

   Ⓑ $25.80

   Ⓒ $29.48

   Ⓓ $36.80

4. Reflect point A over the x-axis and label the reflected point B. Then reflect point C over the y-axis and label the reflected point D.

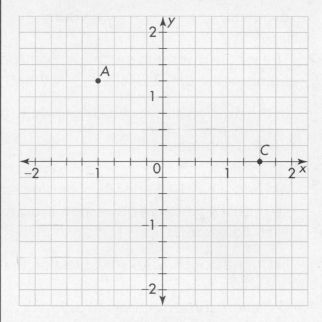

5. On the coordinate plane in Exercise 5, what is the distance between point A and point B?

   _____

6. On the coordinate plane in Exercise 5, what is the distance between point C and point D?

   _____

7. Liam biked on a country road at a constant rate of 12.8 miles per hour. How far did Liam bike in 1.75 hours?

   _____

Name _____

Name _____

ⒶⓏ Vocabulary

1. In a division problem, the **dividend** is the number being divided, the **divisor** is the number by which you are dividing, and the **quotient** is the answer.

   Identify the dividend, divisor, and quotient in the division to the right.

   $$4\overline{)86.72} = 21.68$$

   dividend: _____   divisor: _____   quotient: _____

2. The **whole numbers** are the set of all positive integers and zero. So the whole numbers are 0, 1, 2, 3, 4, 5, 6, 7, 8, 9, and so on.

   In the division above, which is a whole number, the dividend,

   divisor, or quotient? _____

3. Alejandra has 19.8 pounds of potting soil. She wants to divide the soil equally among 4 flowerpots. How much soil will she put in each flowerpot?

   Fill in the box to write an expression to represent this problem.   19.8 ☐ 4

4. Use compatible numbers to estimate the quotient.

   19.8   ÷   4
    ↓   ↓

   _____ ÷ _____ = _____

5. Find the quotient. Fill in the boxes at the right as you complete the steps to divide.

   Divide 19 ÷ 4. Multiply.
   Subtract. Bring down the tenths.

   Divide 38 ÷ 4. Multiply.
   Subtract. Annex a 0 to the dividend. Bring down the hundredths.

   Divide 20 ÷ 4. Multiply. Subtract.

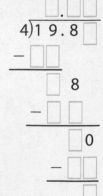

6. Alejandra will put _____ pounds of potting soil in each flowerpot.

7. Is the answer reasonable? Explain. _____

   _____ .

On the Back!

8. Find the quotient 37.4 ÷ 4.

R 7·5

Display the Digit

Get Started

Show the missing digits in the dividend.
Display each 0–9 tile exactly once.
If you have a partner, take turns.

a.
```
      2.18
   4)□.7□
    -8
      7
     -4
      3 2
     -3 2
        0
```
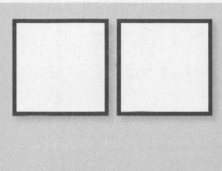

b.
```
      7.8
   8)□2.□
    -56
      6 4
     -6 4
        0
```

c.
```
     18.2
   5)□1.□
    -5
     4 1
    -4 0
       1 0
      -1 0
         0
```

d.
```
      1.09
   7)□.6□
    -7
      6
     -0
      6 3
     -6 3
        0
```

e.
```
     0.83
   7)□.8□
    -5 6
      2 1
     -2 1
        0
```

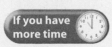
If you have more time

Make up other division puzzles like these.
Ask your partner to display the answers with 0–9 tiles.

Center Game ★ 7·5

Display the Digit

Get Started 👤 or 👥

Show the missing digits in the divisor, dividend, or quotient.
Display each 0–9 tile exactly once.
If you have a partner, take turns.

a.
```
        1 6.3
    □)□ 7.8
     -6
      3 7
     -3 6
        1 8
       -1 8
          0
```

b.
```
          2.□2
    11)□3.3 2
      -2 2
        1 3
       -1 1
           2 2
          -2 2
             0
```

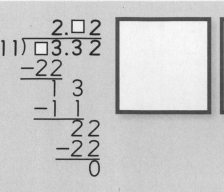

c.
```
       0.5□3
    □)2.5 15
    -2 5
        1
       -0
        1 5
       -1 5
          0
```

d.
```
        3.5□
    □)25.0 6
     -2 1
        4 0
       -3 5
          5 6
         -5 6
            0
```

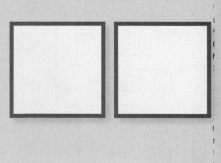

e.
```
        6.□4
    □)25.3 6
    -2 4
       1 3
      -1 2
         1 6
        -1 6
           0
```

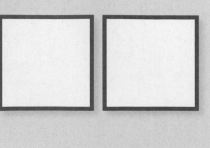

If you have more time 🕐

Make up other division puzzles like these.
Ask your partner to display the answers with 0–9 tiles.

Center Game ★★ ⬤**7·5**

Name _____

1. Find the quotient.

$131.25 \div 15$

Ⓐ 0.875

Ⓑ 8.7

Ⓒ 8.75

Ⓓ 87.5

2. What is the product of $4,639 and 0.25?

Ⓐ $159.75

Ⓑ $900.00

Ⓒ $1,159.30

Ⓓ $1,159.75

3. Lisa spends $8.65 each week on school lunches. How much money does Lisa spend on school lunches in 16 weeks?

Ⓐ $13.51

Ⓑ $43.25

Ⓒ $135.10

Ⓓ $138.40

4. Which inequality is true?

Ⓐ $-5.72 > -5.712$

Ⓑ $-5.715 > -5.709$

Ⓒ $-5.705 < -5.712$

Ⓓ $-5.71 < -5.709$

5. How much more expensive is the 12-pound bag than the 5-pound bag?

Rice	
5-pound bag	$7.95
12-pound bag	$15.48

_____

_____

6. The formula $d = \frac{n(n-3)}{2}$ can be used to find the number of diagonals for a polygon with n sides. Use the formula to find the number of diagonals, d, for a hexagon (6 sides) and a decagon (10 sides).

_____

7. Latisha works at a job that pays $14 per hour. If she earned $1,764 last month, how many hours did she work?

_____

8. Evaluate the expression $\frac{80 - 5x}{3}$ for $x = 4$.

_____

Name _____

Vocabulary

1. A **power of 10** is the product that is the result of raising 10 by an exponent. The exponent and the number of zeros in the power of 10 are equal.

   Complete each equation by finding the power of 10.

   $10^2 =$ _____ $10^{\boxed{}} = 10{,}000$

   $10^6 =$ _____ $10^{\boxed{}} = 100{,}000{,}000$

2. Hyo spent $48.84 for a brisket that costs $3.70 per pound. How much did the brisket weigh?

   Write an expression to solve this problem.

   _____

3. What is the least power of 10 by which you can multiply

   3.7 to get a whole number? _____

   Multiply the divisor and the dividend by the power of 10.

   $3.7 \times$ _____ = _____

   $48.84 \times$ _____ = _____

4. Divide 488.4 by 37. Place the decimal point for the quotient above the decimal point in the dividend.

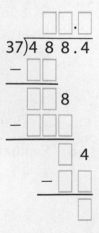

5. So, Hyo bought a _____ pound brisket.

On the Back!

6. Find the quotient $0.9\overline{)4.68}$.

Teamwork

Partner Talk
Share your thinking while you work.

 **Get Started**
 or

Get paper and a pencil.
Put ①②③④ in a bag.

Repeat for Each Round

Choose **a**, **b**, **c**, **d**, **e**, or **f**.
Pick a tile. Pick two tiles if your group has only two students.
Do the jobs listed below in order.
To find your job, find the number that matches the tile you chose.

1 Use compatible numbers to estimate the quotient.

2 Multiply the divisor and dividend by a power of ten that makes the divisor a whole number. Explain.

3 Divide the new dividend by the new divisor to find the quotient.

4 Check to see if your quotient is close to your estimate.

☆☆☆ Divide by a Decimal ☆☆☆

a. $6.3 \div 0.9$	b. $36.6 \div 0.6$
c. $5.25 \div 2.5$	d. $4.84 \div 2.2$
e. $0.824 \div 41.2$	f. $1.64 \div 0.04$

 **If you have more time**

If you have $9.00 in quarters, how many quarters do you have? Use steps 1–4 to find out.

Center Game ★ 7·6

Teamwork

 **Get Started** Get paper and a pencil.
or Put ⟨1⟩ ⟨2⟩ ⟨3⟩ ⟨4⟩ in a bag.

Repeat for Each Round Choose **a, b, c, d, e,** or **f**.
Pick a tile. Pick two tiles if your group has only two students.
Do the jobs listed below in order.
To find your job, find the number that matches the tile you chose.

 1 Use compatible numbers to estimate the quotient.

 2 Multiply the divisor and dividend by the same number that makes the divisor a whole number. Explain.

 3 Divide the new dividend by the new divisor to find the quotient.

 4 Check to see if your quotient is close to your estimate.

☆☆☆ Divide by a Decimal ☆☆☆

a. $0.1925 \div 0.55$	**b.** $1.8936 \div 0.09$
c. $7.35 \div 0.007$	**d.** $0.9696 \div 0.24$
e. $6.4168 \div 1.234$	**f.** $4.27 \div 1.22$

 **If you have more time** If you have $17.00 in nickels, how many nickels do you have? Use steps 1–4 to find out.

Center Game ★★ 7·6

Name _____

1. Select all the expressions that have a quotient of 1.2.

☐ $5.52 \div 4.6$

☐ $0.812 \div 0.58$

☐ $82.8 \div 69$

☐ $131.2 \div 82$

☐ $0.564 \div 0.47$

2. Carl bought 1.06 lb of ham, 1.27 lb of turkey pastrami, and 1.18 lb of cheese at the deli. How many more pounds of deli meat did Carl buy than cheese?

Ⓐ 0.97 lb

Ⓑ 1.05 lb

Ⓒ 1.15 lb

Ⓓ 1.39 lb

3. Which point is located in Quadrant IV?

Ⓐ $(-7.85, -2.41)$

Ⓑ $(7.85, -2.41)$

Ⓒ $(-7.85, 2.41)$

Ⓓ $(7.85, 2.41)$

4. Which is the least power of 10 that you can multiply the divisor and dividend by to make the divisor a whole number?

$16.28\overline{)732.6}$

Ⓐ 10^0

Ⓑ 10^1

Ⓒ 10^2

Ⓓ 10^3

5. Solve the equation.

$35z = 3{,}115$

_____

6. Write a rule and an equation to fit the pattern in the table.

p	1	2.5	4	7.5
q	3.5	5	6.5	10

_____

_____

_____

_____

7. Volunteers called 1,955 registered voters for a survey. Each of the 23 volunteers made the same number of calls. How many calls did each volunteer make?

_____

8. Julia bought a dress for $64.59, shorts for $19.25, jeans for $35.80, and a jacket for $53.99.

The sales tax on Julia's total purchase was $10.42. What was the total amount that Julia spent?

_____

A-Z **Vocabulary**

1. **Equivalent fractions** can be used to understand the division of decimals. The division expression 33.3 ÷ 3.7 can be written as a fraction.

   33.3 ÷ 3.7 can be written as the fraction $\dfrac{\boxed{}}{\boxed{}}$.

   To write an equivalent fraction with a whole-number denominator, multiply 33.3 and 3.7 by 10. Complete the equations below to find the quotient.

   $$\frac{33.3}{3.7} \times \frac{10}{10} = \frac{\boxed{}}{37} = \underline{}$$

   Remember to multiply the dividend and divisor by the same power of 10 when dividing decimals.

2. Find the quotient 17.85 ÷ 5.25.

   What is the least power of 10 by which you can multiply 5.25 to get a whole number? _____

   Multiply both the dividend and divisor by this power of 10 and rewrite the division expression.

   17.85 × 100 = _____   5.25 × 100 = _____

   _____ ÷ _____

3. Divide.

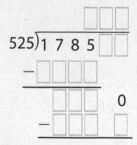

On the Back!

4. Find the quotient 250 ÷ 0.05.

Name _____

1. Which equation represents the graph below?

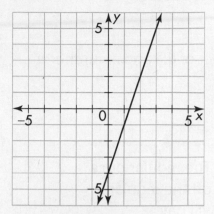

Ⓐ $y = x - 4$

Ⓑ $y = 2x - 4$

Ⓒ $y = 3x$

Ⓓ $y = 3x - 4$

2. Which number represents the same point on the number line as $-(-12)$?

Ⓐ -12

Ⓑ 0

Ⓒ 12

Ⓓ 24

3. Find the quotient.

$0.09\overline{)20.52}$

Ⓐ 2.28

Ⓑ 22.8

Ⓒ 228

Ⓓ 2,280

4. A health club charges $60 to join, plus a monthly fee of $48. What is the total cost for 1 year of membership?

_____

5. John bought 3 boxes of the 14-ounce oat cereal and Bill bought 2 boxes of the 18-ounce oat cereal. How much more did John spend?

6. Four friends went out for lunch. The cost of their meals was $36.80. A tax of $2.94 was added to their bill, and they decided to leave a tip of $7.50. If they divide the final bill evenly, how much should each of them pay?

_____

7. Order these numbers from least to greatest.

$\frac{9}{13}$, $-1\frac{3}{4}$, 0.7, -1.6, $-1\frac{2}{7}$

_____

Name _____

7-8
Reteach to Build
Understanding

🔤 Vocabulary

1. An **algebraic expression**, such as $0.4n \div 2$, uses numbers, variables, and symbols to express a value. Expressions do not include equal signs.

   Write an algebraic expression for each situation.

   7.2 less than a number f The product of 6.4 and a number n

   _____   _____

   The quotient of a number x divided by a number y _____

2. Elena is shopping for several pairs of athletic shorts. The regular price for a pair of shorts is $9.99. Elena has a coupon for $\frac{1}{3}$ off the regular price. Write an expression to find the amount Elena will pay.

   Let $x =$ _____.

3. Write an expression to represent the total cost of the shorts at the regular price.

   _____

4. Write an expression to represent the total cost of the shorts after the coupon is applied.

   The coupon gives $\frac{1}{\square}$ off the regular price, so the sale price is $\frac{\square}{3}$ of the regular price.

   $\frac{\square}{\square}(9.99\underline{\hspace{1cm}})$

5. If Elena buys 5 pairs of shorts using the coupon, how much will she pay?

   Evaluate $\frac{2}{3}(9.99x)$ by substituting _____ for x.

   $\frac{2}{3}\left(9.99 \times \boxed{}\right) = \frac{2}{3} \times \boxed{} = \frac{\boxed{}}{3} = \boxed{}$

6. Elena will pay $ _____ for the shorts.

On the Back!

7. Evaluate $13.2a$ for $a = 7.1$.

Copyright © Pearson Education, Inc., or its affiliates. All Rights Reserved. 6

1. Evaluate the expression for $x = 2.6$.

$x^2 + 3x - 1$

Ⓐ 8.36

Ⓑ 13.56

Ⓒ 14

Ⓓ 15.56

2. Haley bought 3.5 pounds of cherries, 2.6 pounds of peaches, 3.4 pounds of broccoli, and 4.8 pounds of green beans. How many more pounds of vegetables did Haley buy than fruit?

Ⓐ 2.1 pounds

Ⓑ 2.3 pounds

Ⓒ 5.6 pounds

Ⓓ 14.3 pounds

3. In October, Matt worked 62 hours at his part-time job. He earned $775. Which equation could **NOT** be used to find Matt's hourly wage, w?

Ⓐ $62w = 775$

Ⓑ $w = 62 \div 775$

Ⓒ $w = \frac{775}{62}$

Ⓓ $775 \div 62 = w$

4. U-Rent-It charges $45 a day plus $0.65 per mile to rent a small moving truck. Which expression represents the cost in dollars of renting the truck for d days, if it is driven a total of m miles?

Ⓐ $65d + 0.45m$ Ⓒ $45d + 65m$

Ⓑ $45.65m$ Ⓓ $45d + 0.65m$

5. On Monday, the high temperature in Minneapolis was $-8°F$. On Tuesday, the high temperature was $-5°F$. Which day was colder?

_____

6. Estimate the quotient. Then find the exact quotient.

$201.48 \div 2.3$

Estimate: _____

Exact quotient: _____

7. Graph the inequality on the number line.

$x \leq -1$

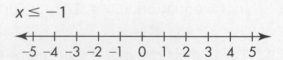

8. Which person's account balance shows a debt greater than $295?

Account Holder	Balance ($)
Katie	374
Steve	-312
Megan	-99
Frank	106

_____

Name _____

Vocabulary

1. **Inverse relationships** are used to solve equations. For example, to solve $2x = 6$ the variable x is isolated by undoing multiplication by 2 with the inverse operation, which is division by 2. So $x = 3$.

   Which operation has an inverse relationship to the operation in the equation and can be used to isolate the variable?

   $y + 4.12 = 12.42$ _____ $x \times 2.4 = 7.2$ _____

   $z \div 9 = 4.1$ _____ $a - 2.3 = 5.4$ _____

2. At the beginning of football practice, one of the water coolers contained 5.2 liters of water. Some water was added to the cooler until it contained 22.1 liters of water. How many times as many liters are there after water is added compared to the beginning amount?

   Solve the equation $5.2x = 22.1$ to find out how many times greater the new amount of water is.

   In the equation $5.2x = 22.1$, the operation of _____ is used.

3. The inverse operation that can be used to get x alone is _____.

4. Solve the equation.

   $$5.2x = 22.1$$

   $5.2x \div$ _____ $= 22.1 \div 5.2$

   _____ $=$ _____

5. So, there was _____ times as many liters of water.

On the Back!

6. Solve the equation $p \div 8.2 = 9.3$ and check your solution.

Think Together

Get Started or

Put `1` `2` `3` `4` in a bag.

For Each Round

Choose A, B, C, D, E, or F.
Pick a tile. Pick two tiles if your group has only two students.
Explain how to solve the equation next to your tile number when it is your turn.
Discuss: Which equations have the same solution?

A Solve each equation.

`1`	$x + 2.5 = 5.8$
`2`	$n + 9.6 = 14.2$
`3`	$h + 22.2 = 44.4$
`4`	$z + 11.7 = 16.3$

B Solve each equation.

`1`	$d - 6.9 = 4.3$
`2`	$c - 18.7 = 9.3$
`3`	$y - 12.7 = 8.6$
`4`	$q - 4.3 = 23.7$

C Solve each equation.

`1`	$w - 27.81 = 14.67$
`2`	$j + 7.96 = 50.44$
`3`	$17.68 = v - 19.23$
`4`	$c + 20.35 = 37.28$

D Solve each equation.

`1`	$2.4v = 16.8$
`2`	$9.7m = 83.42$
`3`	$89.6 = 12.8k$
`4`	$190.4 = 8n$

E Solve each equation.

`1`	$x \div 3.5 = 2.2$
`2`	$v \div 9.6 = 1.5$
`3`	$g \div 13.8 = 1.2$
`4`	$h \div 6 = 2.4$

F Solve each equation.

`1`	$k + 37.28 = 81.75$
`2`	$46.28 = 5.2p$
`3`	$n - 42.39 = 26.88$
`4`	$m \div 3 = 23.09$

If you have more time Make up three equations that have the same solution.

**Think Together**

Partner Talk

Share your thinking while you work.

Get Started
👫 or 👫👫

Put 🔲1 🔲2 🔲3 🔲4 in a bag.

For Each Round

Choose A, B, C, or D.
Pick a tile. Pick two tiles if your group has only two students.
Follow the directions next to your tile number when it is your turn.

A $x + 7.8 = 9.2$

 Solve this equation for *x*. Explain.

 Check your solution.

 Create another equation that has the same solution.

 Create a question that can be answered by solving the given equation.

B $y - 12.74 = 6.29$

 Solve this equation for *y*. Explain.

 Check your solution.

 Create another equation that has the same solution.

 Create a question that can be answered by solving the given equation.

C $25.74 = 4.29b$

 Solve this equation for *b*. Explain.

 Check your solution.

 Create another equation that has the same solution.

 Create a question that can be answered by solving the given equation.

D $z \div 22.6 = 7.9$

 Solve this equation for *z*. Explain.

 Check your solution.

 Create another equation that has the same solution.

 Create a question that can be answered by solving the given equation.

If you have more time

Make up another equation.
Complete steps 1–4 for your equation.

Center Game ★★ **7·9**

Name _____

1. Select all the equations for which $x = 14.8$ is the solution.

   ☐ $x + 9.7 = 25.5$

   ☐ $38.4 - x = 23.6$

   ☐ $7x = 103.6$

   ☐ $35.7 \div x = 2.38$

   ☐ $7.104 \div 0.48 = x$

2. A cell phone plan costs $9.95 per month plus $0.18 per minute of use. Which expression represents the cost in dollars for m months if u minutes are used each month?

   Ⓐ $0.18m + 9.95u$

   Ⓑ $9.95m + 0.18u$

   Ⓒ $18m + 995u$

   Ⓓ $995m + 18u$

3. Melanie bought 12 peaches for $4.68. If p represents the price of one peach, which equation could you solve to find p?

   Ⓐ $12 + p = 4.68$ Ⓒ $\frac{12}{p} = 4.68$

   Ⓑ $12 - p = 4.68$ Ⓓ $12p = 4.68$

4. Find the product.

   68.2×9.85

   Ⓐ 58.35

   Ⓑ 67.177

   Ⓒ 671.77

   Ⓓ $6,717.7$

5. Complete the table.

x	$x + 15$	$2x + 15$	$2(x + 7.5)$
0			
1			
2			
3			

   Which expressions are equivalent?

   _____

   _____

6. Solve the equation. Explain how you got your answer.

   $d \div 0.13 = 47$

   _____

   _____

   _____

7. Evaluate the expression for $z = 5.8$.

   $2z^2 - 3z + 11$

   _____

8. A large bottle of shampoo contains 13.6 fluid ounces. A travel-size container of shampoo holds 1.7 fluid ounces. How many travel-size containers could you fill from the large bottle of shampoo?

   _____

Name _____

Vocabulary

1. Some of the **tools** used to solve math problems include computers, calculators, rulers, and conversion charts.

   Identify a tool that could be used in each situation.

   Multiplying greater numbers: _____

   Finding the number of inches in a mile: _____

   Calculating the area of a textbook: _____

   _____

   Finding the height of the Washington Monument: _____

2. Hanna made 7 quarts of picante sauce. She put the picante sauce in 3.5-ounce jars. What tool can Hanna use to find the number of ounces of sauce that she made?

   [   ]

3. Use the tool you chose in Exercise 2. How many ounces are in 1 quart? _____

   How many ounces of sauce did Hanna make? $7 \times$ _____ = _____

   How many 3.5-ounce jars did Hanna fill?   _____ $\div 3.5 =$ _____

On the Back!

4. Suppose that you can mow a lawn that is 162 square feet using one tank of gas. Is one tank of gas enough to mow a rectangular lawn that is 10.3 feet wide and 14.8 feet long? What tool can help you to solve this problem? Why would you use this tool? Explain how to use this tool strategically to solve the problem.

Name _____

Common Factors and Multiples

Topic 8 Standards

6.NS.B.4

See the front of the Student's Edition for complete standards.

Dear Family,

   Your child is learning about common factors and multiples of numbers. This includes identifying prime and composite numbers and writing the prime factorization of a number. Your child will find the greatest common factor (GCF) of two whole numbers less than or equal to 100 and the least common multiple (LCM) of two whole numbers less than or equal to 12.
   You can help your child strengthen these skills by doing the following activity.

Carnival Fun

Ask your child to find answers for 1 through 10, and to write each answer next to the corresponding number in the story. Have your child read the story aloud.

1. A prime number between 8 and 24.

2. The LCM of 6 and 7.

3. The GCF of 9 and 12.

4. The number of factors of 25.

5. A composite number between 61 and 79.

6. The GCF of 7 and 17.

7. A composite number between 2 and 9.

8. The LCM of 5 and 9.

9. A prime number between 43 and 59.

10. The number of factors of 16.

Francis and Ramona went to a carnival. The price of admission was **1.** _____ dollars. Francis won **2.** _____ toy snakes at the balloon popping booth. Ramona won **3.** _____ goldfish at the coin toss booth. Francis played the test-your-strength game and hit the bell **4.** _____ times. Ramona wanted to ride the Ferris wheel but there were **5.** _____ people ahead of her in line so she decided to use **6.** _____ ticket(s) to guess the number of pennies in a jar. She guessed **7.** _____ pennies and won a giant stuffed panda bear. Francis spent **8.** _____ tickets at the cakewalk booth and won **9.** _____ cupcakes. Just before leaving the carnival, the girls put the rest of their tickets together to buy **10.** _____ hotdogs to eat on the way home. What a fun day!

Observe Your Child

Focus on Mathematical Practice 2

Reason abstractly and quantitatively.

Help your child become proficient with Mathematical Practice 2. Tell your child you are thinking of a number greater than 2 that has exactly 3 factors. Ask your child to explain whether the number is a prime or a composite number.

Factores comunes y múltiplos

Estándares del Tema 8

6.SN.B.4

Los estándares completos se encuentran en las páginas preliminares del Libro del estudiante.

Estimada familia:

Su niño(a) está aprendiendo sobre los factores comunes y los múltiplos de un número. Eso incluye identificar números primos y compuestos y escribir la descomposición en factores primos de un número. Su niño(a) hallará el máximo común divisor (M.C.D.) de dos números enteros menores que o iguales a 100 y el mínimo común múltiplo (m.c.m.) de dos números enteros menores que o iguales a 12.

Ayude a su niño(a) a reforzar estas destrezas con la siguiente actividad.

Diversión en la feria

Pida a su niño(a) que halle las respuestas de los ejercicios 1 a 10 y que las escriba junto al número correspondiente en el cuento. Pídale que lea el cuento en voz alta.

1. Un número primo entre 8 y 24.

2. El m.c.m. de 6 y 7.

3. El M.C.D. de 9 y 12.

4. La cantidad de factores de 25.

5. Un número compuesto entre 61 y 79.

6. El M.C.D. de 7 y 17.

7. Un número compuesto entre 2 y 9.

8. El m.c.m. de 5 y 9.

9. Un número primo entre 43 y 59.

10. La cantidad de factores de 16.

Francisca y Ramona fueron a una feria. El precio del boleto era **1.** _____ dólares. Francisca ganó **2.** _____ serpientes de juguete en el puesto de explotar globos. Ramona ganó **3.** _____ peces en el puesto de lanzamiento de monedas. Francisca jugó a poner a prueba su fuerza y golpeó la campana **4.** _____ veces. Ramona quería ir a la rueda de Chicago pero había **5.** _____ personas en la fila, así que decidió usar **6.** _____ boletos para adivinar cuántas monedas había en un frasco. Dijo que había **7.** _____ monedas y ganó un panda de peluche gigante. Francisca gastó **8.** _____ boletos en el puesto de baile y ganó **9.** _____ bizcochitos. Antes de irse de la feria, las niñas combinaron los boletos que les quedaban para comprar **10.** _____ *hot dogs* que comieron camino a casa. ¡Qué día divertido!

Observe a su niño(a)

Enfoque en la Práctica matemática 2
Razonar de manera abstracta y cuantitativa.

Ayude a su niño(a) a adquirir competencia en la Práctica matemática 2. Dígale que está pensando en un número mayor que 2 que tiene exactamente 3 factores. Pídale que explique si el número es primo o compuesto.

Name _____

Prime Protection

Did You Know? Prime numbers are used to generate public keys that are used to encrypt private information, like personal data and bank and credit card account numbers. Two very large prime numbers are multiplied together to generate a composite number, or public key, that is difficult to factor. The prime factors are the private keys and are the only keys that can be used to access or decode the encrypted data.

Public Key RSA-210 = 2452466449 0027821197651766357308801846 7026787678332759743414451715 0616008300385872169522083993 3207154910362682719167986407 9776723243005600592035631246 5612184658179041001318592996 1993381701214933503487587055 1067

▶ Multiplying a prime number between 300 and 310 by another prime number between 707 and 710 generates an encryption key used to encode a message. What are the two private keys and the encryption key?

_____

2 The relatively weak security key 13191623 was used to encrypt personal data. Multiplying two prime numbers less than 4,000 generated the code. There are 550 prime numbers less than 4,000. Explain how you can break the code.

_____

_____

3 If you know that 3,307 is one of the prime factors used to generate the encryption key in Problem 2, what is the other private key you need to decode the message? Explain how you know.

_____

_____

4 **Extension** Generate your own encryption key by multiplying two prime numbers. Use the Internet and other technology to find prime number factors greater than 10,000.

_____

Name _____

Cicadas

> **Did You Know?** Periodical cicadas live underground most of their lives. Some cicadas emerge every 13 years, and some emerge every 17 years. When cicadas emerge, they find and climb a vertical surface, latch on, and shed their exoskeleton. Adult cicadas come out white and hang upside down overnight as their wings expand and their bodies turn black.

1 Some scientists hypothesize that cicadas emerge in 13-year and 17-year cycles in order to avoid the years when predator populations are at their peak. These "population booms" are directly related to the life spans of the predators. Birds are natural predators of cicadas. Research the bird predators listed below and record each life span.

Predator	Life Span in Years
American Robin	_____
Mississippi Kite	_____
Wild Turkey	_____

2 Some species of cicadas emerge more often, every 2–5 years. Suppose that one year, a brood of cicadas on a 3-year cycle emerges, and in the same year, the robin population is at its peak. In how many years will the cicadas emerge when the robin is experiencing another population boom?

_____

3 A brood of cicadas with a 5-year cycle emerged in the same year that the wild turkey experienced a population boom. Some scientists believe that as a result, wild turkeys were well fed and reproduced at record rates. In how many years is this likely to happen again?

_____

4 **Extension** A brood of 13-year cicadas emerged in the same summer of 1998 that a brood of 17-year cicadas emerged. In what year will this rare occurrence happen again? Explain.

_____

_____

Name _____

1. Divide.

$49\overline{)45{,}391}$

Ⓐ 926

Ⓑ 926 R7

Ⓒ 926 R17

Ⓓ 927 R17

2. Which point is located between
−5.42 and −5.43 on a number line?

Ⓐ −5.4

Ⓑ −5.41

Ⓒ −5.5

Ⓓ −5.427

3. The 13 businesses in a shopping
center each pay an equal share of
the center's electric bill. This month,
they used 2,769 kilowatt-hours of
electricity. How many kilowatt-hours
must each business pay for?

Ⓐ 210 kilowatt-hours

Ⓑ 213 kilowatt-hours

Ⓒ 240 kilowatt-hours

Ⓓ 243 kilowatt-hours

4. Which ordered pair represents the
reflection of the point $Q\left(7\frac{3}{8},\ -5\frac{4}{7}\right)$
across the *y*-axis?

Ⓐ $\left(-7\frac{3}{8},\ -5\frac{4}{7}\right)$

Ⓑ $\left(-7\frac{3}{8},\ 5\frac{4}{7}\right)$

Ⓒ $\left(-5\frac{4}{7},\ 7\frac{3}{8}\right)$

Ⓓ $\left(5\frac{4}{7},\ 7\frac{3}{8}\right)$

5. Evaluate the expression for the
values of *p*.

p	0.1	0.8	2.5	10
$2.05p + \dfrac{5}{p}$				

6. Round to the nearest whole number
to estimate the difference. Then find
the exact difference.

$831.4 - 692.9$

Estimate: _____

Exact difference: _____

7. Emma buys a book and gives the
clerk $13.00. How much did the book
cost if her change is $0.33?

_____

8. Explain how to get the variable alone
on one side of the equation. Then
solve the equation.

$4.85r = 58.2$

_____

_____

Name _____

ᴬ⁻ᶻ Vocabulary

1. A composite number can be written as a product of its prime factors, called its **prime factorization**.

   Circle the prime factorization of 8:   1 × 8   2 × 4   2 × 2 × 2

2. A **factor tree** is a diagram that shows the prime factorization of a composite number.

   Circle the prime factorizations shown in the factor trees.

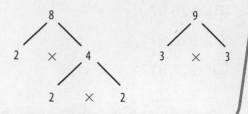

Find the prime factorization of 28.

3. The number 28 is a product of the factors 1 × 28, 2 × _____, and _____ × 7.

   List all the factors of 28: 1, 2, _____, 7, _____, _____.

4. Write 28 as a product using the least prime factor from its list of factors.

   28 = _____ × 14

5. 14 is a composite number, so write its prime factorization.

   First, list all the factors of 14: 1, _____, _____, _____.

6. Continue to write the prime factorization of 28 by writing the least prime factor of 14 from its list of factors.

   28 = _____ × 14

   = _____ × _____ × _____

   Write the prime factorization of 28: _____ × _____ × _____ or $2^2 × 7$.

7. Use a factor tree to write the prime factorization of 12.

   The prime factorization of 12 is 2 × _____ × _____ or $2^\square × 3$.

On the Back!

8. Find the prime factorization of 18. If it is prime, write *prime*.

1. Ed had to make a part for his bulldozer. He started with a piece of metal 1.725 inches wide then he added metal that increased the width by 0.4 inch. Then he ground off some metal so that the width decreased by 0.12 inch. How wide was the piece of metal when Ed finished?

   (A) 2.125 in.

   (B) 2.025 in.

   (C) 2.005 in.

   (D) 1.650 in.

2. Which number is to the right of 2.314 on a number line?

   (A) 2.31   (C) 2.315

   (B) 2.30   (D) 2.313

3. Dimitri drew a line from point $W(-2, 4)$ to point $X(5, 4)$. He drew a second line from point $X(5, 4)$ to point $Y(5, -3)$. What is the combined length of the two lines Dimitri drew?

   (A) 18 units   (C) 7 units

   (B) 14 units   (D) 3 units

4. Which value from the set below is the solution of the equation?

   $327.8 + q = 456.1$

   128.3, 139.3, 783.9

   (A) 128.3

   (B) 139.3

   (C) 783.9

   (D) No solution is given in the set of values.

5. Complete the table for the equation $y = \frac{1}{2}x + 3$.

x	y
0	
2	
4	
6	

6. Use the table data from Exercise 5 to graph the equation $y = \frac{1}{2}x + 3$.

   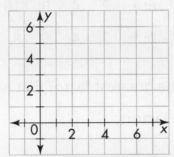

Amanda earns $12.75 per hour working at her local public library.

7. Write an equation that describes the relationship between the time Amanda works, t, in hours, and the amount she earns, e, in dollars.

   _____

8. Amanda worked 23 hours last week. How much did she earn?

   _____

Name _____

Vocabulary

1. The greatest number that is a factor of two or more numbers is the **greatest common factor**, or **GCF**.

   Factors of 8: **1**, **2**, **4**, 8

   Factors of 12: **1**, **2**, 3, **4**, 6, 12

   Common factors of 8 and 12: 1, _____, and _____.

   The _____ of 8 and 12 is 4.

Find the greatest common factor (GCF) of 16 and 40.

2. The factors of each number are listed below. Circle the common factors.

   Factors of 16: 1,   2,   4,   8,   16

   Factors of 40: 1,   2,   4,   5,   8,   10,   20,   40

3. Choose the greatest factor that is common to both numbers.

   Common factors: 1, _____, _____, _____

   GCF = _____

4. The GCF can also be found using prime factorization. The prime factorization of each number is shown below. Circle the prime factors that the two numbers have in common.

   Prime factorization of 16: $2 \times 2 \times 2 \times 2$

   Prime factorization of 40: $2 \times 2 \times 2 \times 5$

   Each prime factorization has 2 as a common factor _____ times.

5. Multiply the common prime factors to find the GCF.

   GCF = 2 × _____ × _____ = _____

On the Back!

6. Find the GCF for 18 and 30.

Name _____

1. Select all the pairs of numbers for which the greatest common factor is 6.

- ☐ 24 and 36
- ☐ 18 and 30
- ☐ 12 and 42
- ☐ 30 and 45
- ☐ 72 and 78

2. A high school band raised $2,615 to buy new drums. If each drum costs $84, how many drums can the band buy?

Ⓐ 30

Ⓑ 31

Ⓒ 32

Ⓓ 33

3. Which equation best represents the data in the table?

m	0	5	10	15
n	3	5	7	9

Ⓐ $n = m + 3$

Ⓑ $n = \frac{5}{2}m + 3$

Ⓒ $n = \frac{2}{5}m - 3$

Ⓓ $n = \frac{2}{5}m + 3$

4. Which expresses $28 + 70$ as a multiple of the sum of two whole numbers with no common factor?

Ⓐ $2(14 + 35)$

Ⓑ $7(4 + 10)$

Ⓒ $14(2 + 5)$

Ⓓ $1(28 + 70)$

5. The table shows how much Alec spent for lunch at school each day last week.

Day	Amount
Monday	$4.55
Tuesday	$5.30
Wednesday	$3.80
Thursday	$4.25
Friday	$3.95

What is the total amount that Alec spent for his lunches at school last week?

_____

6. Angela and Joe mailed their wedding invitations. Each invitation required $0.70 in postage plus $0.34 for the enclosed reply postcard. If they spent a total of $192.40 in order to mail the invitations, how many invitations did they mail?

_____

7. Evaluate the expression for $x = 5$, $x = 10$, and $x = 15$.

$$\frac{180 - 12x}{5}$$

_____

Name _____

Vocabulary

1. A **multiple** is the product of a given factor and any whole number.
   A **common multiple** is a multiple common to two or more numbers.

   Multiples of 2: 2, 4, **6**, 8, 10, **12**, 14, 16, **18**,…
   Multiples of 6: **6**, **12**, **18**,…

   Three common multiples of 2 and 6 are: 6, _____, and _____.

   The **least common multiple** (LCM) is the common multiple with the least value.

   LCM of 2 and 6: _____.

Find the least common multiple of 6 and 9.

2. A few multiples of each number are listed below. Circle the
   multiples the numbers have in common.

   Multiples of 6: 6,   12,   18,   24,   30,   36,…

   Multiples of 9: 9,   18,   27,   36,…

3. Choose the least multiple that is common to both numbers.

   Common multiples: _____, _____

   LCM of 6 and 9: _____

4. Prime factorization is another way to find the LCM.

   Write the prime factorization of each number. Circle the greatest
   number of times each different factor appears.

   Prime factorization of 6:   2 × _____   ⟵ The factor 2 appears _____ time.

                                                   The factor 3 appears _____ time.

   Prime factorization of 9: _____ × _____   ⟵ The factor 3 appears _____ times.

5. To find the LCM, find the product of the factors you circled.

   _____ × _____ × _____ = _____

   LCM of 6 and 9: _____

On the Back!

6. Find the LCM of 8 and 6.

Name _____

1. Select all the numbers that are common multiples of 4 and 6.

- ☐ 8
- ☐ 12
- ☐ 32
- ☐ 72
- ☐ 90

2. A warehouse ships 856 boxes of detergent. The warehouse uses cartons that each hold 24 boxes of detergent. How many cartons are used for the shipment?

- Ⓐ 34
- Ⓑ 35
- Ⓒ 36
- Ⓓ 37

3. Mara buys 2 sandwiches for $5.95 each and 3 drinks for $1.75 each. There is no sales tax. If she pays with a $20 bill, how much change does she receive?

- Ⓐ $2.85
- Ⓑ $4.60
- Ⓒ $8.80
- Ⓓ $12.30

4. What is the greatest common factor of 65 and 90?

- Ⓐ 5
- Ⓑ 10
- Ⓒ 13
- Ⓓ 18

5. Complete the table for the equation $y = \frac{x}{5} + 9$. What happens to the value of y when the value of x increases by 5?

x	y
0	
5	
10	

_____

_____

6. Use the greatest common factor and the Distributive Property to find the sum. Show your work.

$85 + 34$

_____

_____

7. Sam packs lunches for his son Ben. Each lunch includes a juice box and a bag of carrots. He buys the juice boxes in packs of 12 and the carrots in packs of 8 single-serve bags. What is the least number of packs of each that he can buy to have the same number of servings of juice and carrots in each lunch?

_____

_____

Name _____

Vocabulary

1. A **counterexample** is an example that shows that a statement is not true. Write a counterexample for the statement below.

   Statement: All even numbers are composite numbers.
   Example: 4 is a composite number.

   Counterexample: 2 is a(n) _____ number that is

   not a(n) _____ number.

Clara's Bagels ships bagels in boxes of 54 or 72. The bagels are put into plastic bags, then boxed. Clara wants to put the maximum number of bagels in each bag and claims that each bag should contain 6 bagels. Her work is shown below.

Prime factorization of 54: $2 \times 3 \times 3 \times 3$

Prime factorization of 72: $2 \times 2 \times 2 \times 3 \times 3$

GCF of 54 and 72: $2 \times 3 = 6$

2. How does Clara support her claim?

   To find the GCF, Clara multiplied the common _____ factors

   _____ and _____ .

3. Does Clara's math support her claim that the maximum number of bagels each bag should contain is 6? Explain.

   _____ . Clara overlooked a pair of _____ prime factors, so 6 is not the GCF of 54 and 72.

4. Use a counterexample to justify your answer.

   In the box above showing Clara's work, circle the common prime factors that Clara overlooked.

   GCF of 54 and 72: _____ $\times$ _____ $\times$ _____ = _____

   Each bag should contain _____ bagels.

On the Back!

5. Peter says that every square number less than 100 has an odd number of factors. Is there a counterexample that proves his conjecture is not true? Explain.